MAD WORLD

MAD WORLD

War, Movies, Sex

SLAVOJ ŽIŽEK

OR Books
New York · London

© 2023 Slavoj Žižek

Published by OR Books, New York and London
Visit our website at www.orbooks.com

All rights information: rights@orbooks.com

First printing 2023

Library of Congress Cataloging-in-Publication Data: A catalog record for this book is available from the Library of Congress.
British Library Cataloging-in-Publication Data: A catalog record for this book is available from the British Library.

Typeset by Lapiz Digital.

paperback ISBN 978-1-68219-449-2 • ebook ISBN 978-1-68219-450-8

CONTENTS

INTRODUCTION:

THE TRIUMPH OF TECHNO-POPULISM

This book brings together a selection of my columns and commentaries from the last year. The madness evoked in its title is not meant simply as the everyday expression we often use, but as a more precise indication that we live in an epoch in which we miss what Fredric Jameson called "cognitive mapping," a global orientation of where we are and where we move. Years ago, we were dreaming about a post-ideological world—now we have it, and the absence or irrelevance of explicit ideologies makes things even worse.

How did we come to this point? The main shift is that the opposition between center-Left and center-Right parties as the main axis of our political space has been replaced by the opposition between a big technocratic party (standing for expert knowledge) and a populist opponent with anti-corporate and anti-financial motifs. However, this shift underwent another surprising turn. What we have witnessed lately is something one can only call techno-populism: a political movement with clear populist appeal (working for the people, for their "real interests," neither Left nor Right), promising to take care of everyone through rational expert politics, a matter-of-fact approach that doesn't mobilize low passions or resort to demagogic slogans. Academics Bickerton and Accetti write the following on techno-populism:

> Technocratic appeals to expertise and populist invocations of 'the people' have become mainstays of political competition in established democracies. This development is best understood as the emergence of techno-populism—a new political logic that is being superimposed on the traditional struggle between left and right. Political movements and actors combine technocratic and populist appeals in a variety of ways, as do more established parties that are adapting to the particular set of incentives and constraints implicit in this new, unmediated form of politics.[1]

What once seemed the ultimate antagonism of today's politics—the struggle between liberal democracy and right-wing nationalist populism—has miraculously transformed into a peaceful coexistence. Are we dealing

1   Christopher J. Bickerton and Carlo Invernizzi Accetti, *Technopopulism: The New Logic of Democratic Politics* (Oxford: Oxford University Press, 2021).

with some kind of "dialectical synthesis" of the opposites? Yes, but in a very specific sense: The opposites are reconciled through the exclusion of the third term, political antagonism, or the political dimension as such. The unsurpassed model is Mario Draghi in Italy, endorsed as the "neutral" and efficient prime minister by the entire political spectrum (with the significant exception of the extreme right-wing neofascists who are saving the honor of politics), but elements of techno-populism are also recognizable in Emmanuel Macron and even in Angela Merkel.

This reconfiguration puts (whatever remains of) the authentic Left into a difficult position. While techno-populism is the very form of today's establishment, of the apolitical "neutralization" and political antagonisms, it should nonetheless sometimes be strategically supported as a lesser evil when immediate catastrophes (Le Pen, Trump, etc.) pose a threat.

The embarrassing paradox we are compelled to accept is that from a moral standpoint, the most comfortable way to maintain one's high ground is to live in a moderately authoritarian regime. We can oppose the regime (softly following the unwritten rule) without really posing a threat to it, so that we can be assured of our upright moral stance without risking a lot. Even if one does suffer disadvantages (some jobs will be out of reach, one can be prosecuted), such minor punishments only provide the aura of a hero. But once full democracy comes, we all enter the domain of disorientation—choices are no longer so clear. For example, in Hungary in the mid-1990s, the liberal ex-dissidents had to make a difficult choice: Should they enter into a coalition with ex-Communists to prevent the conservative Right from taking power? This was a strategic decision where simple moral reasoning was not enough. That's why many political agents in post-Socialist countries long for the old times when choices were clear. In despair, they try to return to the clarity of the past by equating their actual opponent with old Communists. In Slovenia, the ruling conservative nationalists still blame ex-Communists for all present troubles. For example, they claim that the high number of anti-vaxxers is the result of a continuing Communist legacy. At the same time, the Left-liberal opposition claims that the ruling conservative nationalists govern in exactly the same authoritarian way as the Communists did before 1990. The first gesture of a new politics is to fully admit disorientation and to assume responsibility for difficult strategic choices.

So how will the new techno-populist power deal with the enormous problems that lie ahead? And how can we move beyond it (since it ultimately cannot deal with these problems)? In this book I try to provide some answers, but mostly I deal with three facets of our global situation: the Ukraine war; popular culture (Hollywood) as a machine that registers (and mystifies) our social and ideological deadlocks; and different aspects of our global political situation, from China to today's desperate attempts to create artificial scarcity. My hope is that this collection will help at least some readers to think and search for solutions. We can no longer count on the logic of historical progress; we have to act on our own, because, left to its own immanent logic, history is moving toward a precipice.

I
UKRAINE

THE WAR OF
LUMPEN-BOURGEOISIE

In his "The West at War: On the Self-Enclosure of the Liberal Mind,"[2] philosopher Boris Buden approaches the war in Ukraine through a question that may appear naïve—however, the very appearance of naivety is an effect of the ideological triumph of global capitalist liberalism:

> Isn't it ridiculous to talk about revolution today? Isn't the concept totally discredited? Indeed, this is among the greatest ideological achievements of the liberal mind. / What is missing today in the bloody drama in Ukraine is the idea of revolution. Or more precisely: We miss Lenin—a figure who radically challenges the binary logic behind the clash between two normative identity blocs. / . . . our imagination must reclaim the idea of fast and radical change—as a condition for our survival.

Buden then provides an outline of what this could mean for the ongoing war in Ukraine:

2   Boris Buden, "The West at War: On the Self-Enclosure of the Liberal Mind," *e-flux Journal* 126 (April 2022).

What Russia needs today is not a coup d'état that supposedly returns things to normal. It needs a revolution—a Leninist one with genuine revolutionary violence that will not only remove Putin and his clique from power (he deserves the same fate as Nikolai II), but also destroy his entire system of oligarchic crony capitalism, expropriate the criminal expropriators, and call the oppressed of the world to join the struggle. But this is exactly what the West fears most. The system of parliamentary oligarchy that upholds Putin, with its authoritarian and violent character, is not an exclusively Russian invention. It's the system that best serves the interests of the global ruling class today. This is why there has been so much sympathy for Putin among right-wing circles around the world. If Putin dies, someone else will carry his flag onward, not only in Russia but in many other places around the world, including the West.

Buden concludes his vision with the obvious question to which he provides the only appropriate answer: "Does this sound too utopian? Perhaps, but there is no time left for anything else. Unless we reclaim the utopian vision of radical and rapid change, we are doomed." I think he is right on both counts, and the pessimist that I am read these lines as a syllogism: (1) the revolutionary option is utopian; (2) there is no time left for anything else;

so, (3) we are doomed. The most brutal and depressing fact in recent history is that the only case of Buden's imagined scene—a violent revolutionary crowd invading the seat of power—was on January 6, 2021. A crowd of Trump supporters, denying the results of the democratic presidential election, broke into the U.S. Capitol in Washington, D.C. They viewed the election as illegitimate, a theft organized by corporate elites (they were right up to a point!). Left-liberals reacted with a mix of fascination and horror. There was a bit of envy in their condemnation of "ordinary" people breaking into the sacred seat of power, creating a carnival that momentarily suspended our rules for public life. Now, Elon Musk, a Right establishment version of Assange, is releasing "Twitter Files" in a similar way that the past popular protests transformed themselves into the Trumpian attack on Congress—we move from Assange to Musk. Here is a comment from one of Musk's supporters: "Statues torn down. Humiliating renunciations of thought crimes real and fake. Marxism is being pushed on kids to bring back Pol Pot. And [that's] why your work in buying Twitter may be the last way to avoid genocide and civil war."[3]

---

3   Harry Fletcher, "Elon Musk appears to agree that the left are similar to a genocidal dictator," *Indy100*, December 28, 2022, https://www.indy100.com/viral/elon-musk-pol-pot-left.

So does this mean that the populist Right stole the Left's resistance to the existing system through a popular attack on the seat of power? Is our only choice between parliamentary elections controlled by corrupted elites or uprisings controlled by the populist Right? No wonder Steve Bannon, the ideologist of the new populist Right, openly declares himself as the "Right Leninist for the 21st century":

> Bannon's White House adventure was only one stage of a long journey—the migration of revolutionary-populist language, tactics, and strategies from the left to the right. Bannon has reportedly said: "I'm a Leninist. Lenin . . . wanted to destroy the state, and that's my goal too. I want to bring everything crashing down, and destroy all of today's establishment."[4]

While Bannon derides big corporations, which, with apparatuses of the state, control and exploit ordinary working Americans, he had no problem with the Right hiring the notorious Cambridge Analytica (a data analytics firm) to use the most sophisticated AI to secure Trump's victory in 2016. There is more than anecdotal

4   Cihan Tuğal, "The Rise of the Leninist Right," Verso, January 20, 2018, https://www.versobooks.com/blogs/news/3577-the-rise-of-the-leninist-right.

value in this fact: It signals the vacuity of alt-Right populism, which has to rely on the latest technological advances to maintain its popular redneck appeal. But it also signals the fragility of the entire system, which needs the shocks of populist mobilization to survive. This coincidence of the opposites (technological manipulation and populism) is based on the exclusion of the third: the liberal "free" subject who decides after rational deliberation.

So yes, we are doomed. There is no clear way out, but we should always bear in mind that the global capitalist system is even more doomed, approaching its apocalyptic end. The hopelessness is not ours when we are at the mercy of an undefeatable global capitalist machine; the hopelessness is in the very heart of this machine. There is no hope for us within the coordinates of the existing global system. So back to Buden. We have to think in terms of radical change—and to perceive the contours of such a change, we should not be afraid to re-learn the lessons of the past. Here is a surprising example: Hegel's last published text, the 1831 essay "On the English Reform Bill," in which he cautions about a possible socio-historical turn for the worse, at least in Britain. This text is usually perceived as Hegel's anti-democratic warning against parliamentary elections—against the shift from corporate order, in which individuals participate in the social totality only through their role in a particular estate, to the direct access of individuals in the universal order. However, as philosopher Adrian Johnston pointed out, a closer look allows us to propose a different reading. Hegel "depicts a rich rabble of English landowners as having dispossessed the subsistence-farming peasantry":

> Then, while the "English Reform Bill" of the title of Hegel's essay promises democratic gains through the widening of the franchise for British Parliamentary elections, the just-mentioned dispossession process creates a situation in which this "reform" makes it likely that a wealthy *Pöbel* will manipulate a gullible impoverished populace whose poverty leaves them vulnerable to demagoguery and the like. Thus, seeming progress towards greater democracy, through a bad cunning of reason, probably will lead to actual tyranny in the guise of mob rule by a mob itself ruled by the socially irresponsible rich. Hegel ends this essay predicting that this particular piece of English legislation will lead not to a desirable and peaceful reform, but to an undesirable and bloody revolution.[5]

5   Adrian Johnston, "Capitalism's Implants: A Hegelian Theory of Failed Revolutions," *Crisis & Critique* 8, no. 2 (December 2021): 122–181, https://www.crisiscritique.org/storage/app/media/2021-12-13/cc-82-adrian-johnston.pdf.

Johnston is right to read Hegel backward. Although Hegel's doubt about the English Reform Bill is motivated by his vision of a state divided into estates and thus opposed to liberal egalitarianism (each individual can participate in the universal political sphere only through his/her belonging to a specific estate; s/he should have no direct participation in the universality that bypasses the hierarchic order of estates), he foresaw the anti-egalitarian corruption of the universal right to vote, which occurs when the "rich rabble" manipulate the poor, as is the case in today's nationalist populism.

The so-called oligarchs in Russia and other post-Communist countries are another case of rich rabble; they are not even an authentic creative bourgeoisie, rather they are a bourgeois counterpart to what Marx called *lumpen-proletariat*: *lumpen-bourgeoisie*. It was lumpen-bourgeoisie that exploded in post-Communist countries from the late 1980s on, through wild "privatizations," etc. In Slovenia, the exemplary case of a lumpen-bourgeois is the "independent tax adviser" Rok Snežič, a collaborator and friend of Rightist Janez Janša, the current prime minister of Slovenia. Snežič advises Slovene companies on how to move their seat to Republika Srpska (the Serb part of Bosnia), where taxes are lower than in Slovenia, but he is prohibited to enter the territory of Bosnia because of crime allegations against him. Snežič is the main suspect of an investigation into an international money laundering network. While he declared bankruptcy, has no private possessions, and successfully avoids paying a million Euros in taxes, Snežič drives new luxury cars and pays for jumbo road posters. He has no bank account and is officially employed at a company owned by his wife, with a monthly salary of €373.62, paid in cash. But is such a trend toward lumpen-bourgeoisie not a global trend of today's "normal" capitalism? Are figures like Trump and Musk not also lumpen-billionaires? When Jean-Pierre Dupuy wrote that Trump's election "revealed a state of American society that would have remained hidden had Clinton won," he formulates the reason why, in 2016, I supported Trump.[6]

President Volodymyr Zelensky "has said western countries are more concerned with the economic impact of rising energy prices than with the deaths of

6   Jean-Pierre Dupuy, *The War That Must Not Occur* (Redwood City: Stanford University Press, 2023). Incidentally, Dupuy also rejects the notion that Trump is full of narcissistic self-love: "One should rather speak of self-hatred, thinking of Nietzsche's penetrating insight: 'Whoever is dissatisfied with himself is continually ready for revenge, and we others will be his victims . . . '"

innocent Ukrainians as he denounced the latest wave of sanctions against Russia."[7] Well, it took Zelensky a long time to get how global capitalism and democracy really work, despite Russian gas flowing to Europe through Ukraine. Sooner or later we'll need measures usually associated with War Communism—an emergency state in which the government directly controls key areas of production and reproduction, bypassing market rules. Keep in mind that the Russian attack on Ukraine for the global supply of wheat is a double catastrophe: The two states are not just the greatest exporters of wheat in the world, but also the main sources of chemical fertilizers for Europe, and one can only imagine what this could mean for Europe's harvest. To put it brutally, there is only one serious solution: Our states have to act without relying on market mechanisms and directly organize the production of fertilizers. The paradox is that only such War Communism measures can save our freedoms, not the capitalist market, which is the same market that allows Russian gas to flow through Ukraine to

7   Rory Sullivan, "Western nations more concerned about their economies than civilian deaths in Ukraine, says Zelensky," *Independent*, April 7, 2022, https://www.independent.co.uk/news/world/europe/zelensky-western-sanctions-nato-weapons-b2052877.html.

Europe even while the war is ravaging. We should also consider the financial motivations behind the Ukrainian war: the Russian demand that its oil and gas be paid in rubles is a coordinated attempt with China to depose of the U.S. dollar and the euro as global currencies and replace them with the Chinese yuan.

Ukraine will have to realize sooner or later that since Western solidarity is limited by economic interests, it is not enough to just "defend Europe." Ukraine is now quite literally defending Russia from a path of self-destruction imposed by Putin and his oligarchs. Such a stance in no way implies that we should harbor any illusions about the true aims of the Russian aggression, which are more and more publicly stated. In a recent comment titled "What Russia is obliged to do with Ukraine,"[8] Timofey Sergejcev openly formulates that the premise for the Russian genocidal project in Ukraine is grounded in the fact that the "Nazification" of Ukraine is a European project, and "therefore the denazification of Ukraine is also its inevitable de-Europeanization":

8   Тимофей Сергейцев, "Что Россия должна сделать с Украиной," РИА Новости, last updated May 4, 2022, https://ria.ru/20220403/ukraina-1781469605.html. For an English translation, see https://ria.ru/20220403/ukraina-1781469605.html.

Denazification is necessary when a significant part of the people – most likely the majority – has been mastered and drawn into the Nazi regime in its politics. That is when the hypothesis "the people are good – the government is bad" does not work. Denazification is a set of measures in relation to the Nazified mass of the population, which technically cannot be subjected to direct punishment as war criminals . . . lustration, publication of the names of accomplices of the Nazi regime, involving them in forced labor to restore the destroyed infrastructure as punishment for Nazi activities (from among those who will not be subject to the death penalty or imprisonment) . . . the name "Ukraine" apparently cannot be retained as the title of any fully denazified state entity in a territory liberated from the Nazi regime. Denazification will inevitably also be a de-Ukrainization – a rejection of the large-scale artificial inflation of the ethnic component of self-identification of the population of the territories of historical Little Russia (Malorossiya) and New Russia (Novorossiya), begun by the Soviet authorities . . . The Bandera elite must be liquidated, its re-education is impossible. The social "bog" which actively and passively supported it by action and inaction, must survive the hardships of the war and assimilate the experience as a historical lesson and atonement for its guilt.[9]

Sergejcev not only compares Ukrainian politics with Nazism, he even claims that "ukronazism" carries not less, but a greater threat to the world and Russia than German Nazism of the Hitlerite version. "The name 'Ukraine' apparently cannot be retained as the title of any fully denazified state entity in a territory liberated from the Nazi regime." As it is more than clear from the quoted lines, what Russia plans to do with Ukraine is exactly what Brecht describes in his poem "The Solution," apropos the 1953 popular uprising in the German Democratic Republic:

> After the uprising of the 17th of June / The Secretary of the Writers' Union / Had leaflets distributed on the Stalinallee / Stating that the people / Had forfeited the confidence of the government / And could only win it back / By increased work quotas. / Would it not in that case be simpler / for the government / To dissolve the people / And elect another?

According to Sergejcev, this is what Russia has to do with Ukraine: dissolve the Ukrainian people and elect/create

---

9   Сергейцев, "Что Россия должна сделать с Украиной."

another people. If we read this madness with Putin's claim that Lenin invented Ukraine as a nation, we arrive at the conclusion that, for Putin's ideologists, Ukraine has two fathers: Lenin (who invented it) and Hitler (i.e., the Nazis who inspired "ukronazis" to actualize Lenin's invention). So what does this imply for the geopolitical situation of Russia? In this case, Sergejcev is quite clear, the true target is the West:

> Russia has a high potential for partnerships and allies with countries that the West has oppressed for centuries and which are not going to put on its yoke again. Without Russian sacrifice and struggle, these countries would not have been liberated. The denazification of Ukraine is at the same time its decolonization, which the population of Ukraine will have to understand as it begins to free itself from the intoxication, temptation, and dependence of the so-called European choice.[10]

In short, for Sergejcev, the solution is a radical shift in Russian foreign politics, away from the West and toward nations that have been brutally exploited by Western powers. Russia should take its new place as the leader of the global process of decolonization in all its new forms.

10   Ibid.

The brutal exploitation of Third World countries by Western powers is, of course, a truth that should never be forgotten. However, it is a bit strange coming from Russia, whose history over the last few centuries is one of colonizing expansion: the whole of Siberia up to Alaska, and then down to Northern California, south-eastern Ukraine, which was conquered by Catherine the Great, Kazakhstan, Azerbeijan, Georgia; and now Ukraine will be decolonized by way of Russian colonization! It will be liberated against the will of the majority of its people, who will have to be re-educated to accept colonization as decolonizing liberation.

If global war is avoided, the peace will be fragile, and a looming prospect of war will fund gigantic new military investments in order to maintain the fragile peace. What makes the peace fragile is not just a conflict of economic interests, but also a conflict of interpretations of the Ukrainian war, which is not just a conflict about facts. Faith thus overrides any knowledge of facts, which means that, from the standpoint of the "Russian truth," there are no brutalized corpses in Bucha and elsewhere in Ukraine—it is all staged by Western propaganda.

The time has come for the West—convinced that Putin and Zelensky meeting will be a step toward mutual recognition—to cease obsessively demanding such.

Eventual negotiations should be done coldly, between lower-level bureaucrats—Putin and his inner circle should be ignored as much as possible, treated as criminals we are ashamed to even mention. Ultimately, it is the duty of the Russians themselves to see to this.

In old Yugoslavia, policemen were the butt of jokes; they were seen as stupid and corrupted. In one joke, a policeman returns home unexpectedly and finds his wife alone in bed, half-naked and aroused. He suspects a lover is hiding beneath the big bed, gets on his knees and looks beneath. After a couple of seconds, he stands up with a satisfied expression, mumbling, "Everything okay, nobody is there!" while quickly pushing a couple of banknotes into the pocket of his trousers. This is how accepting poverty and misery in our daily lives is paid by the misery of some form of surplus-enjoyment. In the case of Russia, the suffering of ordinary Russians is paid, not by banknotes, but by cheap patriotic pride of re-establishing Russian greatness. At a press conference on February 7, 2022, Putin noted that the Ukrainian government didn't agree with his demands, after which he said: "Like it or not, it's your duty, my beauty." The saying has well-known sexual connotations: Putin appeared to be quoting from "Sleeping Beauty in a Coffin" by the Soviet-era punk rock group Red Mold: "Sleeping Beauty in a coffin, I crept up and fucked her. Like it or dislike it, sleep, my beauty."[11] Although the Kremlin press representative claimed that Putin was referring to an old folkloric expression, the reference to Ukraine as an object of necrophilia and rape is clear.[12] Russian people will have to realize that they, not the Ukrainians, are the true beauty who is being raped by those in power in Russia.

11 КРАСНАЯ ПЛЕСЕНЬ, "Красная Плесень - Чтобы гость не уходил | Лучшие песни," YouTube, June 25, 2020, video, 2:59, https://www.youtube.com/watch?v=DvPVfgjfhRg.

12 Nathan Hodge, "Putin's use of crude language reveals a lot about his worldview," *CNN*, February 8, 2022, https://edition.cnn.com/2022/02/08/europe/putin-coarse-remarks-ukraine-intl/index.html.

UKRAINE IS LIKE THE WEST BANK, NOT LIKE ISRAEL

Over a decade ago my son and I were eating lunch at a large table when I asked him if he could pass me the salt. He responded, "Of course I can," and did nothing. When I repeated my request, he snapped back with childish impudence: "You asked me if I can do it, and I answered. You didn't tell me that I should really do it!" Who, in this situation, was more free: me or my son? If freedom is understood as freedom of choice, then my son was more free—he had the additional choice of how to understand my question, either literally (am I able to do it) or in the usual everyday sense (a request posed as a question out of politeness). Imagine a world where most people acted like my son: We would never know for sure what someone wanted to say, and we would lose immense amounts of time trying to interpret it.

Have we not been facing a similar situation in our political lives for the last few decades? Even when Donald Trump and his alt-Right populists do not violate explicit laws, they ignore the unwritten rules and customs. Two years ago, in Slovenia, my own country, there was a conflict concerning the nomination of Slovene members of the European court. The Rightist government took its purely formal function literally and acted as if it had to decide and make a choice—like my son who took my request for him to pass the salt literally and didn't do it.

Trump's Republicans are doing something similar in the U.S. The American legal system stipulates that if the outcome of a state's elections is not clear, that state's congress can directly nominate electors. The Republican interpretation of this is that if a Republican-dominated congress does not like an electoral result, it can directly nominate electors. One of the conditions of political democracy is that all political agents speak the same language—meaning there is a common understanding of electoral rules so that electoral outcomes are accepted. If not, we find ourselves close to a civil war, as is now the case in the U.S.

The same holds for international politics: All parties are expected to speak the same language when it comes to freedom and occupation. Today's extreme case is, of course, Russia—claiming its invasion of Ukraine is decolonization. Unfortunately, Ukraine fell into the same trap. In his speech before the Israeli Knesset on March 22, 2022, Zelensky said: "We are in different countries and in completely different conditions. But the threat is the same: for both us and you, the total destruction of the people, state, culture. And even of the names: Ukraine, Israel." I fully agree with political scientist Asad Ghanem, who claims that this speech was:

> . . . a disgrace when it comes to global struggles for freedom and liberation, particularly of the Palestinian people. You reversed the roles of occupier and occupied. You missed another opportunity to demonstrate the justice of your cause and the broader cause of freedom. I am angry and sad that Russia is seeking to occupy your country and to crush the rights of the Ukrainian people to self-determination and freedom, and I believe that every possible support must be given to Ukrainians as they resist this barbaric aggression.[13]

Again, I fully agree with Ghanem that "every possible support must be given to Ukrainians." Western help to Ukraine was not a failure, it stopped the Russian advance—without it, Ukraine would be fully occupied

13   Asad Ghanem, "Dear President Zelensky, your support
        for Israel is a disgrace," *Middle East Eye*, March
        22, 2022, https://www.middleeasteye.net/opinion/
        russia-ukraine-war-israel-palestine-zelensky-support-disgrace.

by Russia. But, unfortunately, Zelensky's Knesset speech was not a singular event: Ukraine regularly takes public positions in support of Israeli occupation. In 2020, it opted to quit the United Nations Committee on the Exercise of the Inalienable Rights of the Palestinian People, a body tasked with supporting Palestinian rights.[14] On August 7, 2022, the Ukrainian ambassador to Israel, Yevgen Korniychuk, expressed his full support for Tel Aviv: "As a Ukrainian whose country is under a very brutal attack by its neighbor, I feel great sympathy towards the Israeli public."[15]

This comparison between Israel and Ukraine is misplaced. If there is a parallel, it is between Ukrainians and West Bank Palestinians. Similar to how Russians treat Ukrainians, Israel denies Palestinians are a nation, they are dismissed as part of the Arabs. The difference is that both Israel and Palestine admit to each other's otherness, whereas Russia claims Ukrainians don't exist—they are

---

14   "Ukraine leaves UN committee on Palestinians," *Israel Hayom*, August 8, 2020, https://www.israelhayom.com/2020/01/08/ukraine-leaves-un-committee-on-palestinians/.

15   "Ukraine Declares Support for Israel, Condemns Palestinian 'Terrorism,'" *Palestine Chronicle*, August 7, 2022, https://www.palestinechronicle.com/ukraine-declares-support-for-israel-condemns-palestinian-terrorism/.

part of Russia and their autonomy is a fiction attributed to Lenin and Nazis. Like Israel, Russia is a military superpower colonizing a smaller and weaker entity (the West Bank and Ukraine, respectively). Like Russia in occupied Ukraine, Israel is practicing a politics of apartheid that reduces Palestinians to second-class citizens.

To add insult to injury, Israel hasn't returned the favor and supported Ukraine. It oscillates between Russia and Ukraine, with a tilt toward Russia for strategic reasons: Israel needs Russia, the patron of Syria, to tolerate its attacks on parts of Syria. Plus, Israel is suspicious of anti-Semitism in Ukraine. Why, then, does Ukraine support Israel? For ideological reasons (and also for winning the West's favor), Ukraine presents its struggle as a defense of Europe and European civilization, and against the barbaric-totalitarian East. It ignores the dark side of Europe, which is marked by modern slavery, colonialism, and Fascism, to name a few.

It is absolutely crucial to formulate the defense of Ukraine in universal terms. If we reduce the Ukrainian struggle to the defense of Europe, we are speaking the language of Putin's court philosopher, Aleksandr Dugin, who opposes Russian and European truths. This has catastrophic implications: It directly serves Russia's global propaganda, which presents its attack on Ukraine as Ukraine's decolonization, as the struggle against Western neoliberal domination, and as a step toward a multipolar world.

Europe and Russia are not speaking the same language. Russia is enforcing new "freedoms" that justify brutal neo-feudal domination. Ukraine is not doing the same. However, by perceiving Israel's colonization of the West Bank as a defensive struggle for freedom, Ukraine is putting its own justified struggle for freedom in the same category as another country's aggression. Sooner or later, Ukraine will have to decide whether it will be truly European, participating in the universal emancipatory project that defines Europe, or part of the neoconservative populist wave.

Back to the anecdote about my son and salt. When Ukraine asked the West, "Can you help me and pass me some arms?" the West replied correctly, offering help instead of the cynical quip, "Yes, I can!" followed by nothing. West Bank Palestinians are also asking for help, but are getting close to nothing, mostly empty statements of solidarity—and sometimes not even that, and instead, solidarity with their oppressor. They ask for the salt, and it's given to their opponent.

CASTRATION HERE AND THERE, CASTRATION EVERYWHERE

Since the beginning of the war for Ukraine, President Zelensky repeatedly addressed Russian soldiers in Russian, promising them safety and decent treatment if they were captured or surrendered to the Ukrainian Army. In stark contrast to this stance is what Gennadiy Druzenko, the owner of a war zone mobile hospital in Eastern Ukraine, said on Ukraine-24 TV channel on March 21, 2022:

> He instructed his medical staff to "castrate captured Russian soldiers" because they are "cockroaches, not people," Russian news agency RT reports. "Trust me, Putin's military hardware burns well. The corpses of 'Putinoids' may stink, but they become unthreatening," he said, according to RT. Druzenko, a constitutional lawyer-turned-volunteer frontline medic, apologized for his words after receiving death threats. In a short Facebook post, Druzenko took back his words and added a screenshot that appears to be a threat addressed to him. He said his hospital "does not castrate anyone

and is not going to. Those were the emotions. I'm sorry. We are saving lives. Period."[16]

The immediate reaction to this news should be: Is this how Ukraine defends Europe? Even the apology is ambiguous. Druzenko apologized after receiving death threats, as if doing it just to protect his life, not because he sincerely changed his mind and understood the horror of what he said. Such ideas should be unambiguously condemned, and any comparative "understanding" (in the style of "this is a minor incident compared to the Russian Army's mass murder") is obscene. We should also look closely at the Ukrainian side, because here we get hints at what Ukraine will be if it retains its independence. For example, in 2019, Ukraine's State Committee on Television and Radio Broadcasting banned the translation of *The Book of Thieves* by Swedish historian Anders Rydell in a Putinian style. The decree claimed the book's appearance would be

---

16 Patricia McKnight, "Ukrainian Medic Apologizes After Saying Russian POWs Should Be Castrated," *Newsweek*, March 22, 2022, https://www.newsweek.com/ukrainian-medic-apologizes-after-saying-russian-pows-should-castrated-1690301. Video clip of this interview available here: https://www.dailymail.co.uk/news/article-10636597/Ukrainian-doctor-tells-TV-interviewer-ordered-staff-CASTRATE-Russian-soldiers.html.

"inciting ethnic, racial, and religious hatred." How? The ban is because of Rydell's critical analysis of the actions of Symon Petliura, a nationalist whose troops murdered countless Jews in pogroms.[17] There are other dark signs, like the prohibitive measures applied on the Ukrainian Left, as if it is automatically pro-Putin.[18]

Such critiques should in no way undermine or limit our commitment to Ukrainian freedom. Plus, it would be easy to find dozens of similar obscene statements and acts on the Russian side. For example, Aleksandr Dugin insisted that Russia should have intervened much earlier, at least after the Maidan events (the large protests on the main square in Kyiv in February 2014, which overthrew the pro-Russian government of Viktor Yanukovych). Missing that opportunity "is the sign of profound, profound hatred of our president of the violence . . . he hates the war . . . Putin is liberal democrat, he is very Western in his opinion, he is very careful about global rules . . . that means he has no other solution in his very liberal

17   "Ukraine commits statue-cide," *BBC*, February 24, 2014, https://www.bbc.com/news/blogs-magazine-monitor-26321963.

18   Volodya Vagner, "Is Zelenskyy Cracking Down on the Ukrainian Left?" *Novara Media*, March 24, 2022, https://novaramedia.com/2022/03/24/is-zelenskyy-cracking-down-on-the-ukrainian-left/.

democratic, globalist almost, vision of the world."[19] With "liberal democrats" like this, who needs neo-Nazis?

The reason I mention the incident with the Ukrainian medic is because of an interview with the pro-Putin movie director Emir Kusturica who, believe it or not, declared *I* was the inspiration for the Ukrainian medic's threat. Here are his exact words: "We saw how the other day a Slovene philosopher inspired the Ukrainian doctor and said that all prisoners should be castrated . . . that the imprisoned Russians should be castrated."[20] Let's clarify this accusation. In my first reaction to the Russian invasion, I mentioned castration and rape, but my source was Putin himself. Back in 2002, Putin replied to a Western journalist's question with: "If you want to become a complete Islamic radical and are ready to undergo circumcision, then I invite you to Moscow. We are a multidenominational country. We have specialists in this question [circumcision].

---

19   "Question 1 – Alexander Dugin," YouTube. This video is no longer available.

20   Emir Kusturica, "Istinu je moguće postići samo naukom," interview by Ljubinka Milinčić, YouTube, March 23, 2022, video, 37:46, https://www.youtube.com/watch?v=tXcfo_uAfSs&t=457s. Here is the Serb original: "Videli smo da je neki dan jedan slovenački filozof inspirisao ukrajinskog doktora i rekao da treba da se kastriraju svi zarobljeni. . . da se zarobljeni Rusi kastriraju."

I will recommend that they carry out the operation in such a way so that afterward, nothing else will grow." This is a rather vulgar threat of castration. And rape? The source is Putin again. During the press conference on February 7, 2022, Putin noted that the Ukrainian government does not like the Minsk agreement and then added: "Like it or not, it's your duty, my beauty." A clear reference to rape.

In accusing me of advocating the castration of Russian soldiers, Kusturica is referring to my comment in the *Spectator* magazine.[21] True, in the conclusion of my article, I recommend that the international community carries out a "castrative" operation on Russia (and to a certain extent, the U.S.!) that entails ignoring and marginalizing the two countries. You might debate whether my metaphor is too provocative, but two things are clear. I borrowed the analogies of castration and rape from Putin, and I do not propose castration of real people but a "castrative operation," the meaning of which I specify as international isolation. And I include the U.S. because to some degree, they are also to blame for the situation in Ukraine.

21   Slavoj Žižek, "Was Russia's 'rape' of Ukraine inevitable?"
      Spectator, February 24, 2022, https://thespectator.com/topic/
      russia-rape-ukraine-inevitable/.

IS THE IDEA OF A UKRAINIAN ORGY REALLY THAT MORBID?

In October 2022, news outlets reported that more than fifteen thousand Ukrainians were organizing a mass orgy in the event that Putin launched a nuclear attack on the war-torn nation. Those potentially participating were asked to decorate their hands with stripes to denote their sexual preference. For example, four stripes meant oral sex and three meant anal sex.[22]

The reaction of the Ukrainians who signed up to join the orgy is noteworthy: "It's the opposite of despair. Even in the worst-case scenario, people will look for something good. That's the mega-optimism of Ukrainians." In the interim, other groups have organized similar events, such as an orgy on Derybasivska Street in Odessa.[23] The notion of a collective orgy is a life-affirming project in a

22 Yaron Steinbuch, "Ukrainians plan apocalyptic orgy in event of Putin launching nuke," *New York Post*, October 6, 2022, https://nypost.com/2022/10/06/ukrainians-plan-orgy-in-event-of-putin-launching-nuke/.

23 Sophia Smith Galer, "Ukrainians Are Responding to the Threat of Nukes By Organising an Orgy," *Vice*, October 4, 2022, https://www.vice.com/en/article/93anx3/ukraine-orgy-russia-nuclear.

time of extreme despair. There is no need for a "deeper" pseudo-Freudian analysis of the disintegration of civilized social links during traumatic times.

Once again, I was ashamed of my own nation after I read Slovenia's representative of scientific research, Dr. Matjaž Gams, commenting on Ukraine's alleged reaction to Putin's nuclear threat as "strange and morbid." Gams argued that when a civilization enters a period of decay, "strange, morbid ideas" appear, like the idea of the mega-orgy promoted by some Ukrainians.[24] So the "strange, morbid" thing is a big orgy (strictly based on consent, etc.) as a reaction to the indistinct Russian destruction of civil infrastructure, and not the destruction itself?

On October 18, 2022, Dmitry Peskov, Putin's press secretary, said that the territories of Ukraine adopted by Russia "are inalienable parts of the Russian Federation," and therefore were protected. "Their security is provided for at the same level as the rest of Russia's territory."[25]

24 Roman Kuhar, "Orgija v Ukrajini," *Delo*, October 18, 2022, https://www.delo.si/mnenja/kolumne/orgija-v-ukrajini/ (in Slovene).

25 Maryam Zakir-Hussain, "Putin places nuclear umbrella over annexed Ukraine regions," *Independent*, October 18, 2022, https://www.independent.co.uk/independentpremium/world/ukraine-putin-nuclear-annexed-regions-b2206107.html.

This claim implies that since Ukraine controls parts of the territories under a nuclear umbrella, it deserves a nuclear attack. No wonder thousands of people on online betting sites are betting that Russia will carry out a nuclear attack this year.[26] What gives additional credibility to this threat is that Russia ordered the city of Kherson (almost entirely encircled by Ukrainian forces) to leave so that it could be hit by a nuclear bomb if Ukraine takes it. Everything seems permitted in the struggle against those called "Satanists" by Putin—the term, used regularly in Russian media, has to be taken seriously. Aleksey Pavlov, assistant secretary of the security council of the Russian Federation (later fired from this post), was calling for the "desatanization" of Ukraine, saying that there were "hundreds of sects" in the country where Orthodox values have been abandoned. "I believe that, with the continuation of the special military operation, it becomes more and more urgent to carry out the desatanization of Ukraine. Using internet manipulation and psycho-technologies, the new regime turned Ukraine from a sovereign state to a

26 James Bickerton, "Will Russia Use Nuclear Weapons? Thousands Are Betting On It," *Newsweek*, October 18, 2022, https://www.newsweek.com/will-russia-use-nuclear-weapons-thousands-are-betting-it-1752837.

totalitarian hypersect."[27] Putin echoed the same stance: "This is a complete denial of humanity, the overthrow of faith and traditional values. Indeed, the suppression of freedom itself has taken on the features of a religion: outright Satanism." No wonder Patriarch Kirill, the head of the Russian Orthodox Church, called Putin "a fighter against the Antichrist" and "chief exorcist."[28] And no wonder, on the same day, Russian lawmakers agreed to toughen the country's discriminatory law against so-called same-sex "propaganda." Russia moved closer to banning all Russians from promoting or "praising" homosexual relationships or publicly suggesting that they are "normal."[29] Some people ask how Russia, still a "normal" state, can ally itself with the "fundamentalist" Iran, but we can see now that, if anything, Russia is more fundamentalist than Iran.

27   Isabel Van Brugen, "Putin Appointed 'Chief Exorcist' as Kremlin Whips up Satanic Panic," *Newsweek*, October 26, 2022, https://www.newsweek.com/putin-chief-exorcist-kremlin-desatanization-ukraine-security-council-1754912.

28   Ibid.

29   Angela Dewan, "Russian 'gay propaganda law' discriminatory, European court rules," *CNN*, June 20, 2017, https://edition.cnn.com/2017/06/20/europe/russia-gay-propaganda-law-ruling/index.html.

When the Russian foreign minister Sergey Lavrov accused the U.S. and NATO of "direct involvement in the Ukraine war," the West's answer should have been: There is only one foreign country directly involved in the Ukraine war, and it is Russia, which is why Ukraine has the full right to strike inside Russia. The sad thing is that the U.S. seems to obey a limitation imposed by Russia: "[The] U.S. secretly altered Himars rockets it gave Ukraine so they couldn't be fired into Russia."[30] But on December 6, 2022, it was reported that Ukrainian forces had used drones to strike two air bases hundreds of miles into Russian territory, prompting military commentators to admit that Zelensky's forces could have managed to cross over the border.[31] "Russia fears Moscow is under attack"—Ukrainians don't have to fear, Kyiv *is* under permanent rocket attack. Putin warns that

---

30   Rozina Sabur, "US secretly altered Himars rockets it gave Ukraine so they couldn't be fired into Russia," originally published in the *Telegraph*, December 5, 2022, available here: https://www.msn.com/en-gb/news/world/us-secretly-altered-himars-rockets-it-gave-ukraine-so-they-couldn-t-be-fired-into-russia/ar-AA14VeBx?ocid=msedgntp&cvid=bb5e1923d9cf40d68ce70d2062edff8d.

31   Tom Watling, "Russia fears 'Moscow is under attack' as Ukraine strikes Putin's airfields," *Daily Express*, December 6, 2022, https://www.express.co.uk/news/world/1705760/Russia-military-air-bases-missile-strikes-drone-attacks-ukraine-war.

anyone attacking Moscow will be "wiped out,"[32] while Russian forces are already wiping out not only Kyiv, but Ukraine's entire infrastructure.

Ukraine is now the victim of a new type of war. The battlefield is more or less stable, but Russia is systematically destroying the civilian infrastructure of the entire country. Russian playwright Anton Chekhov wrote: "Any idiot can face crisis; it's this day-to-day living that wears you out." His remark is appropriate for the Ukrainian war. Ukraine is becoming like Palestine. Palestinian painter Sliman Mansour said that ordinary daily life for Palestinians is political, part of political-military struggle.[33] The same politicization of daily life goes on in Iran—what is more ordinary than wearing a scarf or not? And in Ukraine, what is more ordinary than to turn on electricity or fill a glass with water from a pipe?

But what is even more morbid is that Russia's brutality is the idea of some "Leftist" peaceniks who think

---

32 Arpan Rai and Jane Dalton, "Ukraine-Russian news – live: Putin warns anyone attacking Moscow will be 'wiped out,'" *Independent*, December 9, 2022, https://www.independent. co.uk/news/world/europe/ukraine-russia-putin-war-moscow-warning-b2242486.html.

33 Aljaž Vrabec, "Nisem videl nobenih Angelov. Nič ni, nič . . . Samo tema," *Delo*, December 3, 2022, https://www.delo.si/ sobotna-priloga/nisem-videl-nobenih-angelov-nic-ni-nic-samo-tema/.

now is the time to send a big European delegation to Russia to inquire and negotiate about the terms of peace. We, the authentic Left, should do everything possible to prevent a new world war, beginning with a ruthlessly realist evaluation of what Russia is today. We should abandon Eurasian stupidity, i.e., the idea that only a pact between Europe and Russia could bring about a new power bloc that would in turn enable Europe to avoid the fate of being a minor partner of the U.S. in the forthcoming conflict with China. At this point, Russia is simply more dangerous than China.

Russia wants Europe to pressure Ukraine to accept a compromise with Russia, so the West should not negotiate with them, but also shouldn't ignore the people in Russia who oppose the war. In this regard, Ukrainian leadership is making a mistake. Polish journalist Sławomir Sierakowski noticed that "an alliance between the Ukrainian administration and the Belarusian opposition therefore seems natural. Unfortunately, nothing of the kind has emerged . . . Consider the reaction from Mykhailo Podolyak, an important adviser to Zelensky, following news that this year's Nobel Peace Prize would be shared by the Belarusian human-rights advocate Ales Bialiatski, the Russian NGO Memorial, and the Ukrainian Center for Civil Liberties. He tweeted: 'Nobel Committee has an interesting understanding of word "peace" if representatives of two countries that attacked a third one receive @NobelPrize together. Neither Russian nor Belarusian organizations were able to organize resistance to the war.'"[34]

As Sierakowski points out, this is not only morally wrong but also politically stupid. Russian opponents of the war are called traitors by Putin's establishment, and Russians by Ukraine, which leaves them in a strange predicament. In this way, the meaning of the Ukrainian war is obfuscated. It is not a struggle between "European truth" and "Russian truth," as both Dugin and some Ukrainians claim; it is a case of the global struggle against the new nationalist fundamentalism which is gaining strength everywhere, in Russia and in the U.S., in India and in China. If there is anywhere that Ukrainians have ceded a sliver of moral high ground, it is here, not in any Dionysian dissipation outside Kyiv.

34 Sławomir Sierakowski, "Why Is Ukraine Rejecting Its Natural Allies?" *Project Syndicate*, October 18, 2022, https://www.project-syndicate.org/commentary/ukraine-zelenksy-government-spurning-belarusian-natural-allies-by-slawomir-sierakowski-2022-10.

AM I NOW ASHAMED OF ONCE PUBLISHING IN *RUSSIA TODAY*?

No, absolutely not! Here is the main reason.

While our attention was focused on the Ukrainian war, a news item went largely unnoticed. On April 20, 2022, Julian Assange moved one step closer to being extradited to the U.S., to be tried under the Espionage Act. A London court issued a formal extradition order in a hearing, leaving UK Home Secretary Priti Patel (who proposed sending refugees who arrived in the UK to Rwanda) to rubber-stamp his transfer to the U.S. If convicted, Assange faces up to 175 years in prison.[35] So yes, we should fully support Ukrainian resistance, and yes, we should defend Western freedoms—imagine what would have happened to Chelsea Manning if she were a Russian! But our Western freedom also has limits, and we should never lose sight of its boundaries, especially in moments like these.

35 Rob Picheta and Amy Cassidy, "Julian Assange extradition order issued by London court, moving WikiLeaks founder closer to US transfer," *CNN*, April 20, 2022, https://edition.cnn.com/2022/04/20/uk/julian-assange-extradition-order-intl/index.html.

People are demanding that Putin be brought to the International Criminal Court (ICC) to be tried for Russian war crimes in Ukraine. Okay, but how can the U.S. make this demand while refusing to be a member of the ICC? And, to add insult to injury: How can the U.S. demand the extradition of Assange to the U.S. when he is neither an American citizen nor was he involved in spying on the U.S.? All Assange did was make U.S. war crimes public. Recall, for example, the famous video clip of U.S. snipers killing Iraqi civilians. Assange could receive 175 years in prison for simply disclosing indisputable U.S. crimes, which are not even inclusive of the long list of crimes committed by U.S. presidents! If Putin belongs at the Hague, why not also Assange? Why not George W. Bush and Donald Rumsfeld (who is already dead) for the "shock and awe" bombardment of Baghdad? It appears to be a weird reversal of the well-known motto "act globally, think locally." This contradiction was best exemplified in 2003 by the two-sided pressure the U.S. exerted on Serbia. U.S. representatives simultaneously demanded the Serbian government deliver suspected war criminals to the ICC *and* sign a bilateral treaty with the U.S. that would forbid Serbia from delivering U.S. citizens suspected of war crimes or other crimes against humanity to any international institution (i.e., to the

SAME Hague court). No wonder the Serb reaction is one of perplexed fury.

There were topics—not only Assange, but also the weaknesses of liberal democracy, Israeli apartheid politics in the West Bank, the aberrations of Political Correctness—that I frankly was only able to publish in English in *Russia Today*. If I were to publish on a marginal site in the West, the texts would have had limited impact. We have more freedom in the liberal West, but that's why prohibitions are all the more conspicuous. Western democracies also have their dirty side, and their own types of censorship, so the Left has the full right to ruthlessly play one superpower against the other. What I wrote for *Russia Today* and what I am now writing, about my full support of Ukraine, are part of the same struggle—in the same way that there is no "contradiction" between the struggle against anti-Semitism and the struggle against what Israel is doing in the West Bank with Palestinians. If we see Ukraine and Assange as a choice, we are lost; we already sold our soul to the devil. Such a common struggle is not a utopia; what makes it necessary is the deep interconnection of different forms of extreme suffering. In a memorable passage in *Still Alive: A Holocaust Girlhood Remembered*, Ruth

Klüger describes a conversation with "some advanced PhD candidates" in Germany:

> . . . one reports how in Jerusalem he made the acquaintance of an old Hungarian Jew who was a survivor of Auschwitz, and yet this man cursed the Arabs and held them all in contempt. How can someone who comes from Auschwitz talk like that? the German asks. I get into the act and argue, perhaps more hotly than need be. What did he expect? Auschwitz was no instructional institution . . . You learned nothing there, and least of all humanity and tolerance. Absolutely nothing good came out of the concentration camps, I hear myself saying, with my voice rising, and he expects catharsis, purgation, the sort of thing you go to the theatre for? They were the most useless, pointless establishments imaginable.[36]

In short, the extreme horror of Auschwitz did not make it into a place that purified surviving victims into ethical non-egotistical subjects. On the contrary, part of the horror of Auschwitz was that it also dehumanized many of its victims, transforming them into brutal insensitive

36   Ruth Klüger, *Still Alive: A Holocaust Girlhood Remembered* (New York: The Feminist Press, 2003), 189.

survivors unable to make balanced or ethical judgments. The lesson to be drawn here is a sad one: We have to abandon the idea that there is something emancipatory in extreme experiences, that they enable us to clear the mess and open our eyes to the ultimate truth of a situation. Or, as Arthur Koestler, the great anti-Communist convert, put it concisely: "If power corrupts, the reverse is also true; persecution corrupts the victims, though perhaps in subtler and more tragic ways."

NOW is the time to insist on equal treatment and to address the same critical questions to Russia and to the West. We are all Ukrainians in the sense that every nation has the right to defend itself like Ukraine.

MACGUFFIN IN UKRAINE

Some commentators have noted the strange homology between Russia's evocation of secret bioweapon labs in Ukraine and the U.S. evocation of Saddam Hussein's weapons of mass destruction (WMDs). In both cases, these "weapons" justified a military attack. The U.S. knew Hussein did NOT have WMDs, which is why they risked the ground offensive in Iraq. If the U.S. actually believed their own claims that Iraq had WMDs, they probably would not have launched a ground assault for fear of too many casualties. The non-existent "Iraqi weapons of mass destruction" were analogous to the "MacGuffin" in Alfred Hitchcock's films: an object, device, or event that is necessary to the plot and the motivation of the characters, but insignificant, unimportant, or irrelevant itself. Usually, the MacGuffin is revealed in the first act, and its importance wanes thereafter. (Incidentally, one of the most famous Hitchcockian MacGuffins *is* a potential weapon of mass destruction—the bottles with "radioactive diamonds" in *Notorious*!)

Iraqi WMDs were an elusive entity, never empirically specified. After the U.S. invasion of Iraq in 2003, United Nations inspectors were searching for WMDs in Iraq. The weapons were expected to be hidden in the most disparate and improbable places, from the (rather logical) desert to the (slightly irrational) cellars of the presidential palaces. Allegedly, the weapons were in large quantities, yet magically moved all the time. And the more all-present and all-powerful they appeared as a threat, the more they were proclaimed to be destroyed by bombing, as if the destruction of the greater part of the weapons magically heightened the destructive power of the remainder. The fact that the weapons could never be found made them all the more dangerous.

In the case of the Ukrainian war, the MacGuffins are "secret bioweapon labs" in Ukraine, funded and organized by the U.S. These labs supposedly develop poisons that cause human sicknesses, and their destruction is used as the reason for Russia's plan to seize all of Ukraine, as opposed to just the southwestern area where there is a strong Russian minority. But again, I claim Russia positively knows there are no "secret bioweapon labs" full of dangerous poisons in Ukraine. If such labs were there, Russia would have acted with greater urgency—directly attacking these labs or trying to occupy them with elite parachute units.

To avoid a fatal misunderstanding: This does not mean that there are no bioweapons being developed in secret labs—all big countries have them, of course. And the media is right in treating these Russian accusations as a dark hint or threat that they themselves may use bioweapons. The Ukrainian war could take many worse turns, like the use of bioweapons and/or gasses that hinder the functioning of our brains, or a full digital attack on the enemy's cyberspace. We are also not yet in a total breakdown, where it is only "Us" and the "Other" (external and/or internal enemy), and no shared space. The autonomy of the symbolic order (which opens up the space for metaphoric substitutions in which a universal can stand for a particular) is proof that we are far from such a pure struggle. Recall a video that went viral on social media mid-March 2022 of a woman being arrested by the Russian police for holding up a small piece of paper that read "two words" (*два* слова in Russian) which, of course, referred to the forbidden slogan "no to war" (нет *войне* in Russian). At its extreme, absence itself can be "determinate," it can refer to specific content. Russian police also arrested demonstrators who protested with blank signs. A video that received millions of views shows a woman holding a blank sign among a group of people before police officers approach her and escort her away from the crowd.[37] This substitution worked because everybody knew what was prohibited in Russia: to publicly reject the war against Ukraine.

I remember another case of censorship in Communist Czechoslovakia from my youth in the 1970s. During this time, Martina Navratilova was the world's top tennis player. She had immigrated to the West and become a non-person, even for the Czech sports media. When Navratilova was a semi-finalist in an international championship, a Czech sports outlet reported on it without even mentioning her name. The title indicated there were four players in the tournament, they listed three of them, leaving out Navratilova altogether. As weird and primitive as this censorship was, it followed a certain logic: It didn't just obfuscate the truth, because the inconsistency of the title pointed toward the excluded fourth name, which was thus "present in the mode of absence" (to use structuralist jargon).

---

37   Monir Ghaedi, "Russian protesters continue to denounce war, risking arrest," *DW*, April 16, 2022, https://www.dw.com/en/viral-protests-russians-continue-to-denounce-war-risking-imprisonment/a-61143188.

Such censorship is structured like what Lacan calls the "university discourse": knowledge acts as the agent of today's predominant cynical discourse.[38] The object of this knowledge is what Lacan calls *objet a*: the fantasized secret object, WMDs in the case of the U.S. attacking Iraq and of Russia attacking Ukraine. The "product" of this discourse is the agent presumed to threaten us with WMDs (the drug-addicted neo-Nazi Ukrainian leadership). But the truth of this obsession with WMDs is that a paranoiac Master (U.S. leadership, Putin and his circle) concocted the object (WMDs).

The media often reports that two sides of the conflict speak different languages: There is no shared world, there is a "Russian truth" and a "European truth," as Dugin says. In contrast to this prevailing dogma, I think the Ukrainian war fits perfectly within Lacan's formula of (symbolic) communication: In successful communication, I get my own message in its inverted and true form. I say something, but I am not aware of its true meaning—it is only from the catastrophic reaction to my message that I become aware of what my message really amounted to. Say I intervene in a country

38   Jacques Lacan, *The Seminar of Jacques Lacan: The Other Side of Psychoanalysis,* translated by Russel Griggs (New York: Norton, 2007).

for humanitarian reasons, but violent resistance to my intervention makes it clear that my true aim was to dominate the country. From its invasion of Iraq, the U.S. learned the truth about intervention: Iraq is now, more than ever, under the influence of Iran. It is more of an Islamic fundamentalist country than it was under Saddam, and women hold a lower position in public life. The U.S. also got a belated copy of its own war crimes from Russia. Madeleine Albright should be remembered for a *60 Minutes* interview, when interviewer Lesley Stahl asked whether the death of half of million Iraqi children was "worth it." Albright responded: "I think that is a very hard choice, but the price, we think, the price is worth it."[39] Hillary Clinton's pre-electoral campaign against Bernie Sanders reached its lowest point when, campaigning for Clinton, Albright said: "There's a special place in hell for women who don't help each other!" (Meaning: women who vote for Sanders instead of Clinton.) Maybe we should amend this statement: There is a special place in hell for women (and men) who think half a million dead children is an affordable

---

39   Jon Jackson, "Watch: Madeleine Albright Saying Iraqui Kids' Deaths 'Worth It' Resurfaces," *Newsweek*, April 23, 2022, https://www.newsweek.com/watch-madeleine-albright-saying-iraqi-kids-deaths-worth-it-resurfaces-1691193.

price for a military intervention that ruins a country, while wholeheartedly supporting women's and gay rights at home . . . Is Albright's quote not infinitely more obscene and lewd than all Trump's sexist banalities? Was Albright, measured by standards which enable us to proclaim Putin a war criminal, not also a war criminal of at least the same status?

And the same goes for Russia. In one of his lectures in 2022, Dugin said that the attack on Ukraine was Russia's desperate attempt to make its message heard in the West. After twenty years of futile attempts to be heard and considered in a peaceful way, war was the only way left open to Russia. Yes, the Russian message was heard, but the message it got back was that NATO and Europe were unified more than ever against Russia. Russia invaded Ukraine, claiming there is no separate Ukrainian nation, that they are part of the same large ethnic and cultural group, and—at this moment, at least—the result is that the Ukrainian identity is stronger than ever, and that many Ukrainians hate Russians and don't want to have anything to do with them.

THE CURIOUS INCIDENT OF THE MISSING ORBÁN IN KYIV

I fully support Ukrainian resistance, and this partisan view makes me attentive to how, unfortunately, many on the Left try to sit on two chairs regarding the Ukrainian war. Most condemn Russian aggression and simultaneously blame the U.S. for it. For example, the Democratic Socialists of America (DSA) reacted to the war by "calling for the dissolution of NATO's Western alliance and blaming the United States' 'imperialist expansionism' for Russia's unprovoked attack on Ukraine."[40] The DSA is not ready to admit that in spite of the complexity of the situation, Ukrainians are offering a fully justified and heroic resistance to the Russian attack, a resistance that should be unconditionally supported. Instead of this, one hears "Socialist" voices telling Ukrainian workers

40 Elizabeth Elkind, "AOC and Bernie Sanders' 'Democratic Socialists' group blames the US for Russian invasion of Ukraine and demands NATO is scrapped: 'US must end the imperialist expansionism that set the stage for this conflict,'" *Daily Mail*, February 28, 2022, https://www.dailymail.co.uk/news/article-10561299/AOC-Bernies-Democratic-Socialists-group-blames-Russia-invasion-demands-end-NATO.html.

that they should organize against Russian occupiers outside the corrupt government and oligarchs' army. At the end of this road, there is a Leftist conspiracy theory: "The U.S. had its war in Ukraine. Without it, Washington could not attempt to destroy Russia's economy, orchestrate world condemnation, and lead an insurgency to bleed Russia, all part of an attempt to overthrow its government."[41]

In an almost symmetrical way, the liberal Right also doubts that the Left can fully support Ukrainian resistance. Although Putin is definitely not a Leftist, he is, nonetheless, perceived as an ally of some Leftist regimes. No wonder, as in Lacan's formula of communication, the developed West is getting its own message back from the Third World. Countries from Latin America to South Africa are not ready to unanimously condemn Russia for war crimes in Ukraine—they remember much worse crimes committed by the West around the world. That's why their reaction to the demand "defend Europe" is: Why should we defend the power which was doing to us what it now condemns in Ukraine?

41   Joe Lauria, "Biden Confirms Why the US Needed This War," *Consortium News*, March 27, 2022, https://consortiumnews.com/2022/03/27/can-russia-escape-the-us-trap/.

And in some sense, they are right. Europe is also sitting on two chairs. On March 15, 2022, four European leaders made a long, hazardous journey by train from Poland to Kyiv in a show of support as the city came under further Russian attack. The prime ministers of Poland, Slovenia, the Czech Republic, and Hungary met Zelensky as a curfew was mandated in Kyiv. Afterward, Poland's prime minister, Mateusz Morawiecki, tweeted that Ukraine was reminding Europe what courage was—it was time for "sluggish and decayed" Europe to reawaken and "break through her wall of indifference and give Ukraine hope," he wrote.[42] Hungary's prime minister, Viktor Orbán was not one of the four leaders who met that night; the fourth place was occupied by Jarosław Kaczyński, the head of Poland's ruling party and the de facto ruler of Poland.

We all know the famous dialogue from the 1937 film *Silver Blaze* about the "curious incident of the dog in the night-time." Gregory (a Scotland Yard detective) asks: "Is there any other point to which you would wish to draw my attention?"

42 "Ukraine war: European leaders risk train ride to meet Zelensky," *BBC*, March 16, 2022, https://www.bbc.com/news/world-europe-60757157.

Sherlock Holmes responds: "To the curious incident of the dog in the night-time."

"The dog did nothing in the night-time."

"That was the curious incident."

It is easy to replace the dog with Orbán: "Is there any other point to which you would wish to draw my attention?"

"To the curious incident of Viktor Orbán on the train to Kyiv."

"But Orbán was not on that train."

"That was the curious incident." Kaczyński taking the place of the absent Orbán offers the key to the entire affair. It was not just sitting on two chairs; it was one person replacing another on the same chair.

Both Orbán and Kaczyński embody, at their purest, the basic stance of some key members of what is commonly referred as the Visegrád group. The Visegrád group is composed of post-Communist East European countries that are members of the EU but oppose the EU's stance on stronger European unity and cooperation, as well as the cultural values of feminism, multiculturalism, anti-racism, and religious neutrality. Poland and Hungary were, until recently, under pressure from Brussels to abandon their anti-abortion and anti-gay politics and inclination toward authoritarianism. The EU even threatened to withhold financial support to these countries if they did not comply with EU rules. Against this pressure, "illiberal democrats" (like Orbán) promoted national identity and Christian tradition. Both Poland and Hungary have used the burden of the Ukrainian war (taking care of the refugees, etc.) to distract the EU from pressuring them to adhere to human rights standards. On a more general level, we should never forget that ongoing conflicts, wars included, are never just a matter of culture and geopolitics; they are moments of inner tensions in the global circulation of capital. Some signs indicate that even the glorious Maidan event, an authentic student and popular uprising, was (partially, at least) overdetermined by the struggle between two groups of Ukrainian oligarchs and their foreign masters, the pro-Russian clique and the pro-Western clique. The "clash of civilizations" is a truth, but by far not the whole truth.

However, the crux of the matter resides elsewhere. Whichever way you turn it, united Europe does stand for some kind of Social Democracy, which is why in a recent interview Orbán went so far as to proclaim that the Western liberal hegemony "is gradually becoming Marxist."

Sooner or later we'll have to face up to the fact that, opposing the Christian democratic camp, we're no longer dealing with a group espousing liberal ideology, but with a group that's essentially Marxist with liberal remnants. This is what we have in America today. For the time being the conservative side is at a disadvantage in relation to the Marxist, liberal camp.[43]

So why did Orbán not participate in the trip to Ukraine? Because of Hungary's economic links with Putin's Russia, which compelled him to proclaim neutrality in the ongoing Ukrainian war. In a recent public address, Zelensky directly criticized Hungary for this neutrality: "You [Hungarians] must decide whom to side with."[44] So Poland and Hungary decided to play a double game. Two Polish anti-Russian hard-liners went to Kyiv pretending to be there as special envoys of the EU.

43   "Interview with Prime Minister Viktor Orbán in the political weekly 'Mandiner,'" interview by Zoltán Szalai and Gergő Kereki, *About Hungary*, March 3, 2022, https://abouthungary.hu/speeches-and-remarks/interview-with-prime-minister-viktor-orban-in-the-political-weekly-mandiner.

44   Denes Albert, "'I am a lawyer, he is an actor' – Orbán responds to Zelensky's criticism of Hungary's neutrality," *Remix*, March 28, 2022, https://rmx.news/hungary/i-am-a-lawyer-he-is-an-actor-orban-responds-to-zelenskys-criticism-of-hungarys-neutrality/.

No wonder their "mission" caused embarrassment in Brussels; no EU body authorized them to do it. But the actual aim of their mission was not to act in Kyiv on behalf of Europe, but to signal a clear division in Europe. It was a mission directed *against* united Europe. Their message to Ukraine was: We are your only true allies, only we truly and fully support your struggle against the Russian invasion, not the "sluggish and decayed" liberal Western Europe.

All the militant measures advocated by some members of the mission in Kyiv (imposing a no-fly zone over Ukraine, etc.) barely concealed their true aim: to woo Ukraine into their nationalist-illiberal Europe, to strengthen it against the (still hegemonic) Social Democratic Europe. Their mind is on the big question: Where will Ukraine be when the war comes to a close (and the progress of negotiations indicates that some kind of peace is on the horizon)? In this sense, although Orbán was not in Kyiv, his key message was delivered there. And this is why Janša, partisan of radical militancy against Russia, defended Orbán against Ukrainian critique. The visitors knew that their militant proposals would have no consequences: Their battle was not against Putin's Russia but against the Social Democratic ("Marxist," for Orbán) Europe.

Recall Zelensky's call to Hungarians: "You must decide whom to side with."[45] He got a cynical answer from Orbán. In his victory speech, Orbán said: "We never had so many opponents . . . Brussels bureaucrats . . . the international mainstream media, and the Ukrainian president." His mention of Zelensky was accompanied by merry laughter.[46] Now, it is Zelensky and Ukraine who must decide who to side with, which Europe *they* want to be part of.

45   Albert, "'I am a lawyer, he is an actor.'"

46   "Hungary election: PM Viktor Orban criticizes Ukraine's Zelensky as he wins vote," *BBC*, April 4, 2022, https://www.bbc.com/news/world-europe-60977917.

II

HOLLYWOOD

THE VACUITY OF HOLLYWOOD'S MORAL TURN

Lately there have been many falsely progressive movies—ones that illustrate openness to immigrants, the predicament of the nomadic working class, feminine solidarity, etc. But these films deal with these topics in a "decaffeinated" way, blurring their critical edge. Let's take three movies as examples: *Black Widow*, *Luca*, and *Nomadland*.

Black Widow is usually categorized as a meta-genre—Marvel superheroes-meet-Bourne or Bond—but a more pertinent characterization is a Marvel movie made during the #MeToo wave. How is this feminization inscribed into the texture of the film? *Black Widow* is directed by a woman (Cate Shortland), and one can speculate that this accounts for some of the film's #MeToo motifs. The emotional focus of the film is the relationship between Natasha (Scarlett Johansson) and Yelena (Florence Pugh), a sisterly couple engaged in a complex relationship of love and competition, care and suspicion. In a similar vein, the best episode of the film takes place in Budapest, in an ordinary apartment inside a house with crumbling facade.

In a prologue set twenty years earlier, we discover that Natasha and Yelena are not real sisters. In 1995, Russian super-soldier Alexei Shostakov and Black Widow Melina Vostokoff, both Russian undercover agents, posed as a family in Ohio with their surrogate daughters Natasha Romanoff and Yelena Belova. After finishing their mission, they escape back to Russia where General Dreykov (played by Ray Winstone) has Romanoff and Belova taken to the Red Room for training to become Black Widows: perfect killers whose minds are controlled. Even twenty years later, the two sisters long for a proper place in a nuclear family, despite both knowing that the nuclear family they were taken from was fake. Liberation, for them, is not liberation from family ties, but liberation from the wired-brain program that controls them. In their attempt to regain freedom, the two heroines break their "natural" father out of prison so he can help them, but he is now an impotent, aged, and confused clown.

One can argue that the key to the film is the two paternal figures: The father who was imposed on them as their "natural" parent is a weak clown, and his absence is filled by a figure who, instead of exerting symbolic authority over his "children," controls their brains.

One should ask these simple questions: Why are all Dreykov's agents women? And why was the Red Room's chemical agent that enables Dreykov to control women's minds developed by a woman (specifically Vostokoff, the heroines' fake mother)? Does this not indicate that Dreykov, far from being simply an extreme representation of the male fantasy of the total domination over women, is instead a figure of feminine fantasy? This fantasy figure is weak and ineffective—which is why, although Winstone is usually excellent as an evil character, Dreykov somehow doesn't catch on as a bad guy, and the last half hour of the film (the protracted battle against Dreykov) is flat and boring. It is at this point that the film turns wrong: In a time of weakened paternal authority, what prevents women's full emancipation is not (yet) mind-control, but a set of social and ideological conditions. Dreykov as the ultimate enemy is a fetish, a ridiculous mask that obfuscates these conditions.

A similar obfuscation is easily detectable in *Luca* (Enrico Casarosa, 2021). Set on the Italian Riviera in the 1950s–1960s, the film centers on Luca Paguro, a sea monster boy with the ability to assume human form while on land. Luca explores the town of Portorosso with his new human best friend Alberto Scorfano and experiences a life-changing summer.[47] The sea monster is obviously a metaphor for feeling different, from being LGBTQ+ to being an immigrant. This sounds nice, but it is ideology at its worst: In this universe, there are no antagonisms among sea monsters or humans, so all that is needed is trust, friendship, and tolerant understanding.

So what is wrong with *Nomadland* (Chloe Zhao, 2020), which seems to focus precisely on those excluded from the mainstream of our societies? In Germany and some other countries, a vague so-called "classism"—a class version of identify politics—is emerging. In this version of classism, workers are taught to safeguard and promote their socio-cultural practices and self-respect; they are made aware of the crucial role they play in social reproduction. Worker movements thus become another element in the chain of identities, like a particular race or sexual orientation. Such a "solution" to the "workers' problem" characterizes Fascism and populism as respectful to workers and able to admit that workers are often exploited, and they (usually sincerely) want to make workers' position better within the coordinates of the existing system. Trump was doing this, too.

47 Resumed from Wikipedia: "*Luca*," Wikipedia, last modified June 26, 2023, https://en.wikipedia.org/wiki/Luca_(2021_film).

He protected U.S. workers from banks and unfair Chinese competition.

Is *Nomadland* not the ultimate example of such classism? It portrays the daily lives of our "nomadic proletarians," workers without a permanent home who live in trailers and wander around from one temporary job to another. They are shown as decent people, full of spontaneous goodness and solidarity with each other, inhabiting their own world of small customs and rituals, and enjoying their modest happiness. Even the occasional work in an Amazon packaging center goes quite well— that's how our hegemonic ideology likes to see workers. No wonder the movie was the big winner of the 2021 Oscars. Although the lives depicted are rather miserable, the movie bribes us into enjoying it with the charming details of a specific way of life. The movie's tagline could have been: "Enjoy being a nomadic proletarian!"

It is precisely the refusal to be such an element in the chain of identities that defines the authentic workers movement. In India I met with the representatives of the lowest group of the lowest sub-caste of the Untouchables, the dry toilet cleaners. I asked them about the basic premise of their program and what they wanted. They instantly gave me an answer: "We don't want to be ourselves, what we are." Workers are, to quote French philosopher Jacques Rancière, a "part of no-part" of the social body, they lack a proper place in it—an antagonism embodied. Are we asking too much of Hollywood if we expect movies about lives that are a "part of no-part" of our societies? Bong Joon-ho's *Parasite* did it, Todd Phillips' *Joker* did it, and it can be done again.

TÁR'S PARALLAX

The common definition of parallax is the apparent displacement of an object (the shift of its position against a background), caused by a change in the place from which we observe it.[48] The philosophical twist to be added is, of course, that the observed difference is not simply "subjective"—the same object which exists "out there" is seen from two different points of view. It is rather that, as Hegel would have put it, subject and object are inherently "mediated," so that an "epistemological" shift in the subject's point of view always reflects an "ontological" shift in the object itself. In the 1960s and '70s, it was possible to buy soft-porn postcards with a woman in a bikini or wearing a proper gown, and when one moved the postcard or looked at it from a slightly different perspective, the dress would magically disappear and one could see the woman's naked body. This is how things are with the film *Tár*: The heroine's sublime beauty and her monstrous brutality are intimately connected, as in the vulgar postcard. A small shift in our

48   For a more systematic elaboration of the notion of parallax, see my *Parallax View* (Cambridge, MA: MIT Press, 2006).

point of view makes her uncanny nature visible, since her artistic passion is grounded in her very monstrosity.

Recall the famous scene in *Persona* (Ingmar Bergman, 1966) of actress Bibi Andersson talking about the beach orgy and passionate lovemaking in which she participated. In this scene, we see no flashback pictures, and yet it is one of the most erotic scenes in cinema history—the excitement is in how she tells it, a form of "jouissance feminine." Similarly, in Lars von Trier's *Breaking the Waves*, Bess (Emily Watson), a simpleminded and deeply religious girl from a small Scottish town, marries Jan (Stellan Skarsgård), a hearty oil rig worker. After the sexual ecstasy of their honeymoon, Bess can't bear having Jan go back to the rigs, so she begs God to return Jan to her, promising that in exchange, she would put up with any test of her faith. Soon afterward, as if in answer to her prayers, Jan returns, but he is paralyzed from the waist down due to an accident at the oil rig. Confined to his hospital bed, Jan tells Bess she must make love to other men and describe her experiences to him in detail—this way, she will keep awake his will to live. Although she will be doing the act physically with other men, the true sex will occur in their conversation. The same two actors play the leading roles in *Chernobyl* (a 2019 miniseries that revolves around the Chernobyl disaster of 1986 and the cleanup efforts that followed). Skarsgård is Boris Shcherbina, a Council of Ministers deputy chairman who is sent by Mikhail Gorbachev to Chernobyl to provide a truthful appreciation of the catastrophe. Watson is Ulana Khomyuk, a nuclear physicist from Minsk who accompanies Shcherbina and tells him the entire truth, convincing him of the utter seriousness of the situation. There are many scenes in the series where Skarsgård sits in a chair and Watson stands near him, explaining the technical details of what happened in Chernobyl. While I was watching the show, a crazy idea came to me. Wouldn't it be a wonderful provocation if, at some point, Skarsgård, bored by Watson's interminable explanations, interrupted her and said something like, "This is really getting tedious—why don't we do like we did in *Breaking the Waves* and instead, to keep me awake, you describe the details of your latest sexual encounters?" And then, after five or ten minutes of this, the conversation returns to Chernobyl. How would an average viewer react to this? Would such a scene not appear as a parallax shift into another dimension, like moving the postcard to see the naked breasts of a lady? Again, this is what we get in *Tár*.

    Tár (Todd Field, 2022) is a movie about Lydia Tár (Cate Blanchett), a famous composer-conductor and the first female chief conductor of the Berlin Philharmonic. In an interview at the New Yorker Festival, she promotes several new projects, including her upcoming live recording of Mahler's Fifth Symphony. Lydia has lunch with Eliot Kaplan, a conductor who manages a fellowship program she founded for aspiring women conductors, and talks about replacing her assistant conductor, Sebastian, presumably with Francesca, her personal assistant. Later, while Lydia is teaching at the Juilliard School, she ridicules Max, a student, for lacking interest in conducting the classical masters due to identity politics. She encourages students to look past superficial differences to find the music underneath. Max subsequently storms out.

Before returning to Berlin, Lydia receives Vita Sackville-West's novel *Challenge* from Krista Taylor, a former fellowship program member. Dream sequences and email interactions suggest Lydia had groomed Krista into entering a sexually transactional relationship, which later falls apart. Lydia blacklists Krista, ruining her chances at a conducting career. Before a blind audition for a new orchestra cellist, Lydia sees one hopeful candidate, a Russian woman named Olga, in the bathroom. Attracted to Olga, Lydia offers her favors, such as changing her scorecard to ensure a spot in the orchestra and a soloist position in the companion piece to Mahler's Fifth. As Francesca and Sharon (Tár's wife and concertmaster) recognize Lydia's attraction to Olga, their respective relationships are strained. There is an interesting detail about Olga that is regularly missed by critics: Olga is the only woman in the movie not under pressure or terrorized by Lydia. She is a staunch Leftist, and tells Lydia that she regularly participated in Leftist demonstrations in Berlin, mentioning Clara Zetkin (a big name in German Social Democracy), who proposed to establish March 8 as a day of women's rights.

Lydia informs Sebastian of his imminent replacement. Incensed, he indicates the orchestra is aware of her favoritism, and suggests she is guilty of abusive behavior towards young women. Sebastian speculates Francesca will be his replacement, and implies that this is in exchange for sexual favors. Unnerved by the accusations, Lydia decides to replace Sebastian with a different candidate. Krista dies by suicide, leaving a note with serious allegations against Lydia. Lydia instructs Francesca to delete any emails from or about her. Lydia retains a lawyer, as Krista's parents plan to sue her. She is haunted by screaming women in the distance, nightmares, chronic pain, an increasing sensitivity to sound, and enigmatic scribbles resembling those Krista once made.[49] Her only respites are Olga and her adopted daughter, Petra.

One day, after practicing Olga's solo, Lydia follows her home to an abandoned and dilapidated apartment complex. Scared by a dog, Lydia trips and injures herself. She lies to Sharon and her orchestra, claiming the injuries were from an assault. Without telling Lydia, Francesca resigns upon learning she will not be replacing Sebastian. An edited, out-of-context video of Lydia's Juilliard class goes viral, and an article with accusations against her appears in the *New York Post*. Protesters meet Lydia as she returns to New York to promote her book and attend a deposition for Krista's lawsuit. At the deposition, it is implied that Francesca has shared damning emails with the plaintiff. Lydia takes Olga along, but Olga abandons her. Back home, Sharon, furious with the allegations, but more so at Lydia's lack of communication or seeking her counsel as her spouse, leaves with Petra. Lydia is removed as conductor. She sneaks into the live recording performance of Mahler's Fifth and attacks her replacement, Eliot. Advised to lie low by her management agency, she returns to her

---

49   Content resumed from Wikipedia: "*Tár*," Wikipedia, last modified June 26, 2023, https://en.wikipedia.org/wiki/Tár.

lower-class childhood home on Staten Island,[50] where her brother comes home and scolds her, telling her that her birth name is Linda Tarr.

Sometime later, Lydia finds work conducting an orchestra in an unnamed Southeast Asian country. At a massage parlor/brothel where escorts are staged and framed like her orchestra, she picks her masseuse from a big glass bowl. One girl looks up into Lydia's eyes, her bodily posture the same as Olga's, and Lydia rushes outside to vomit. Lydia conducts her new orchestra in the score for the video game series *Monster Hunter* in front of an audience of cosplayers. "We have gone from Mahler's Fifth to a PlayStation 2 game."[51] But she treats the orchestra with the same seriousness and passion as the big philharmonic orchestras of her previous career.[52]

The predominant reading of *Tár* is that it presents a politically correct and pro-cancel-culture monster who pays the price she deserves for brutally exploiting the people around her. The question is how far we go in this

50 Ibid.

51 George Edelman, "'TÁR' Movie Ending Explained," No Film School, December 13, 2022, https://nofilmschool.com/tar-movie-ending-explained.

52 The plot is shamelessly condensed from Wikipedia.

direction: Is Lydia innately an all-devouring monster or is she this way because she has been influenced by the big European tradition of male cis-hetero composers and conductors, from Bach to Mahler? At the opposite end, there are reviewers who found the movie to be a devastating critique of cancel culture and, for this reason, rejected it. For example, Richard Brody described *Tár* as "a regressive film that takes bitter aim at so-called cancel culture and lampoons so-called identity politics," accusing the film of "conservative button-pushing" with a "conservative, and narrow" aesthetic, failing to "forge dramatic unity."[53] Incidentally, for me, it is precisely this lack of dramatic unity, this mixing of genre rules, that makes the film interesting. Then, there are reviewers who also saw the film as targeting cancel culture, but agree with it. George Edelman writes that there are "more than breadcrumbs leading us to the conclusion that through cancel culture, we are canceling culture," and "the final frame implies strongly that culture itself is what's on the chopping block."[54] But then Edelman him-

53 Richard Brody, "'TÁR' Reviewed: Regressive Ideas to Match Regressive Aesthetics," *The New Yorker*, October 12, 2022, https://www.newyorker.com/culture/the-front-row/tar-reviewed-regressive-ideas-to-match-regressive-aesthetics.

54 Edelman, "'TÁR' Movie Ending Explained."

self relativizes this strong claim by way of introducing the prospect of historical change:

> Or is it that culture is simply evolving? And that Lydia Tár's brutal takedown of a young Juilliard student early on was someone too high on the elitist nature of the craft . . . ignoring that the new modern popular versions have their own value . . . one she will eventually come to depend on. You can read *TÁR* several different ways, and that is its true gift.[55]

This reference to historical change avoids the true problem: Of course there is a change, and today we cannot go on composing like Bach, or even like Mahler, but does this fact in any way affect the absolute greatness and genius of their music? One cannot but agree with the final sentence of the last quote: We can read *Tár* in different ways. So, let's move on to yet another reading of the film, according to which, after Tár's fall and escape from the dog, all that happens (including the vision of the dog) are her hallucinations. There is "the *uncanniness* of its final act, the supernatural elements and the hints, more than hints: the big, broad *pronouncements*—that a great deal of what we're seeing on the screen might just

55   Ibid.

be happening inside Lydia Tár's head," writes Dan Kois. Joe Bernstein further provides a very pertinent specification: "A kind of hallucination or dream of personal disgrace, which therapy tells us is secretly pleasurable."[56] The next (and last) step is to project the content of Lydia's hallucinations back into external reality, so that we enter the supranatural domain of a ghost story:

> Reading the "plot" of *Tár* literally is a mistake. For long stretches of the film, we have exited the realm of realism and are firmly in the world of the supernatural. *Tár* is not truly a cancel culture movie. *Tár* is a kind of ghost story, in which we're so deeply embedded in Lydia Tár's psyche that nearly everything that appears onscreen is up for debate.
>
> The ghost, of course, is that of Krista Taylor, Lydia's former protégée, with whom Lydia is accused of sleeping and who, we know, was blackballed from conducting jobs through the

56   Joe Bernstein [@Bernstein], "Ok, I can't keep this promise. I really think the last 30-45 minutes of Tár are a kind of hallucination or dream of personal disgrace, which therapy tells us is secretly pleasurable. Please someone argue with me" *Twitter*, November 16, 2022, https://twitter.com/Bernstein/status/1592972299627810817.

emails Lydia hurries to delete. Even before
Krista's death by suicide, she haunts Lydia.[57]

One cannot help but note that the circle is thus closed:
Lydia is a monster who is haunted by the ghosts of her
victims.[58] The shift from one genre or theme to another
(docu-report, social conflict of mores between patriarchal tradition and cancel culture, psychological drama
of Lydia's inner decay, direct staging of her hallucinations, ghost story) also affects narrative modes. At the
beginning, (too) long conversations and improvisations
about "serious" topics of classical music imitate a documentary or biographical approach, giving the impres-
sion that even if *Tár* is not a documentary, it must be
about a real person. At the film's beginning, we see Adam
Gopnik (a real person who does interviews for *The New
Yorker*) interviewing Lydia for the New Yorker Festival,
simply playing himself. This complex move from semi-
documentary to gothic fiction multiplies parallax into

57   Dan Kois, "*Tár* Is the Most-Talked-About Movie of the Year.
      So Why Is Everyone Talking About It All Wrong?" *Slate*,
      December 8, 2022, https://slate.com/culture/2022/12/tar-cate-
      blanchett-movie-ending-explained-analyzed.html.

58   Martin Milliman, "'TÁR' Is Actually a Horror Movie," *Collider*,
      December 27, 2022, https://collider.com/tar-horror-movie/.

four versions, descending lower and lower into the dark recesses of Lydia's personality. The shift seems to deliver the lesson formulated a century ago by Rainer Maria Rilke in his *Duino Elegies*:

> For beauty is nothing but the beginning of terror which we are barely able to endure, and it amazes us so, because it serenely disdains to destroy us. Every angel is terrible.[59]

However, one should note that *Tár* ignores *this* horror that dwells in the very heart of beauty, and reduces the opposition to one between the sublime beauty of the work of art and the dark (cruel, manipulative, exploitative) side of the author of it. What about the opposite case: a great artist who is privately a very kind and generous person, but his art is full of unspeakable evil?

What makes Lydia such an interesting person is that she is a lesbian but anti-cancel culture. If she were a pro-cancel-culture lesbian, it would have been much more difficult to see her as a monster. The implication of those critical of her is that, although a lesbian, she acts like the oppressive and aggressive patriarchal men whom she admires (from Bach to Mahler). But defenders

59   Rilke, Rainer Maria (1875–1926) - Duino Elegies
      (poetryintranslation.com).

of the position that art cannot be separated from personal identity because it expresses this identity strangely ignore the fact that she is a lesbian: There are lesbian academic figures who are very manipulative and exploitative like Lydia.

As for the relation between art and an artist's life, the movie mentions Gustav Mahler, who was not supportive of his wife, Alma's, compositions—even claiming that one composer was enough for a family. However, after her depression and affair with Gropius, Mahler apologized and started to encourage Alma's composing, even helping her prepare some compositions for publication. Alma had her own problems—although married to a Jew, she was virulently anti-Semitic. As for composers, Richard Wagner, yes, he was openly anti-Semitic, a lying hypocrite, and an opportunist, but a close analysis shows that in his work—which is one of the absolute peaks of world music—he largely overcame his private prejudices. From the opera *The Flying Dutchman* to Wotan as Wanderer in *The Twilight of Gods*, the main hero of Wagner's musical dramas is an eternally wandering Jew. Plus, his caricatural portraits of a Jew (like Mime in Siegfried) are clearly also ironic self-portraits.[60]

60 I developed this point in detail in the following: Mladen Dolar and Slavoj Žižek, *Opera's Second Death* (New York: Routledge, 2001).

Many similar cases demonstrate that a great work of art is eternal in its own way—it is an event *sui generis* that cannot be reduced to its circumstances or conceived as an expression of the personality of the artist. An artist is not just a genius but also an apostle, a medium through which another dimension can speak. Bach is a long-dead cis-hetero white man, but his music is some of the greatest ever. And this holds for all the big names of European classical music. Two decades ago, I was visiting a couple of big Chinese cities and went to pirated DVD stores, where the shelves were full of European classics. I remember I bought a dozen or so versions of Mozart's *Don Giovanni*. Whichever way you turn it, Western classical music really *is* universal—why? In the introduction of *Grundrisse*, Karl Marx openly confronts the problem that accompanies all attempts to historicize works of art, writing that the issue ". . . lies not in understanding that the Greek arts and epic are bound up with certain forms of social development. The difficulty is that they still afford us artistic pleasure and that in a certain respect they count as a norm and as an unattainable model." However, the solution he proposes is not only brutally Eurocentric, but also sustained by Romantic prejudices: "A man cannot become a child again, or he becomes childish. But does he not find joy in the child's naïveté, and must he himself not strive to reproduce its truth at a higher stage? Does not the true character of each epoch come alive in the nature of its children? Why should not the historic childhood of humanity, its most beautiful unfolding, as a stage never to return, exercise an eternal charm? There are unruly children and precocious children. Many of the old peoples belong in this category. The Greeks were normal children. The charm of their art for us is not in contradiction to the undeveloped stage of society on which it grew."[61]

What standard or notion of normality does Marx rely on when he claims that the ancient Greeks were normal children? If Greeks were normal children, who, then, were the *abnormal* children? Jews? Barbarians living around ancient Greece? And what about the ancient Chinese or Egyptians—are they also to be classified as abnormal children, or are they even less than children, totally foreign to our tradition? But if they are foreign to it, how can they also fully enjoy European classical music? Plus, there is the obvious question: If we still enjoy ancient Greek art because "the historic childhood

---

61 Karl Marx, *Grundrisse* (Penguin Books in association with New Left Review, 1973), Marxist Internet Archive, https://www. marxists.org/archive/marx/works/download/pdf/grundrisse.pdf.

of humanity, its most beautiful unfolding, as a stage never to return, exercises an eternal charm," why did the ancient Greeks themselves enjoy it? They certainly didn't perceive *themselves* as normal children.

In his *Philosophy of History*, Friedrich Hegel offers a wonderful characterization of Thucydides's history of the Peloponnesian War. "In the Peloponnesian War, the struggle was essentially between Athens and Sparta. Thucydides has left us the history of the greater part of it, and his immortal work is the absolute gain which humanity has derived from that contest."[62] One should read this judgment in all its naïveté. In a way, from the standpoint of world history, the Peloponnesian War took place so that Thucydides could write a book on it. The term "absolute" should be given all its weight. From the relative standpoint of our finite human interests, the numerous real tragedies of the Peloponnesian War are, of course, infinitely more important than a book; but from the standpoint of the absolute, it is the book that matters. One should not be afraid to say the same thing about some truly great works of art. The Elizabethan era occurred in order to produce

62   G. W. F. Hegel, *Lectures on the Philosophy of History* (London: Henry G. Bohn, 1861), 277.

Shakespeare—Shakespeare's work is "the absolute gain which humanity has derived" from the vicissitudes of his era.

Two points against historicism are to be added here. The "eternity" of a work of art does not mean it should be not related to history, it means that it triumphantly survives being transposed from one cultural and historical context to another, where such a transposition often brings out dimensions absent in the original. Shakespeare is the exemplary case: Each epoch invents its own Hamlet. Recall the best cinema version of the play: *Only Bad People Can Sleep Well*, the 1962 film by Akira Kurosawa set in contemporary Japan. Even more, to understand Shakespeare, we don't need to know the details of the Elizabethan era, whereas the best way to understand the Elizabethan era is to read and watch Shakespeare.

Back to *Tár*. Lydia is depicted as a full artist dedicated to her work and in touch with its "eternal" dimension. She simply is not fully present in our everyday terrestrial reality, so no wonder, when measured by the standards of this reality, her acts often appear unacceptable. I don't see the film's progress as a decline from narcissistic self-infatuation, which makes Lydia blind to her manipulation and exploitation of the people around her, to her gradual confrontation with the consequences of her actions, which leads to her cancellation and exclusion from the Western high art society. I see, in Lydia's commitment to her art, the exact opposite of narcissism: an authentic dedication to her Cause. Yes, she exploits and manipulates her collaborators and partners, but this is part of her ruthless pursuit for her Cause. Plus, the others around her are not as clean as they appear. Why should Sebastian not be replaced as the assistant conductor? Does Francesca really deserve the position promised to her?

Lydia's rejection of cancel culture in the debate with a student about Bach is absolutely justified, and the way the recording of this debate is used in a very manipulative and censored way makes it pure slander. Is all this not proven by the end of the film, when while conducting a cheap orchestra for a music of a video game, Lydia retains the same artistic integrity? She is not broken; she still has a Cause.

After being cancelled, Lydia is shown at her Staten Island childhood home watching a tape of Leonard Bernstein's first episode of Young People's Concerts, "What Does Music Mean?" Like Bernstein over his career as a conductor, Lydia is also focused on recording all of Mahler's symphonies. So, to conclude, let's imagine

Lydia conducting one of Bernstein's lesser-known masterpieces, a concerto for violin, *Serenade after Plato's Symposium* (each of the five movements corresponding to one of the main speakers in *Symposium*: Phaedrus, Aristophanes, Eryximachus, Agathon, and Socrates).[63] If Lydia were to perform this white dead man's concerto dedicated to another long-dead white man's classic text on love, I see absolutely no reason for politically correct suspicions: We should enjoy it without constraints.

63 Violin Express, "Bernstein: Serenade after Plato's Symposium – Alexandra Soumm /Carlos M. Prieto /Detroit Symphony," YouTube, May 22, 2020, video, 33:13, https://www.youtube.com/ watch?v=XsBW9FcjZCs. This is my preferred version. One should note who Alexandra Soumm's parents are (Ukrainian father, Russian mother)—a proper message regarding the ongoing war.

WHY A QUEEN IS BETTER THAN
A WOMAN KING

Four events concerning women took place in 2022: the funeral of Elizabeth II, the electoral victory of Giorgia Meloni in Italy, the release of the movie *The Woman King*, and the widespread protests after the killing of Mahsa Amini in Iran. To understand what is going on in the world today, not just regarding the situation of women, it is necessary to analyze these four events together.

The rise of the New Right governments in Europe—the UK, Sweden, Italy—is not a surprise. It was long coming, as the result of the Left's mistakes, including its failure to provide an adequate answer to the crisis of liberal democracies themselves (obviously, liberal democracy is no longer the political form that enables us to cope with the threat of new catastrophes). But we should bring out another feature of the Right's revival: the important role of women, from Marine Le Pen in France to Giorgia Meloni in Italy. Margaret Thatcher, Sarah Palin, and Priti Patel are no longer eccentricities in the liberal establishment or in the new populist

Right, which has found a way to integrate women who act stronger than masculine technocratic experts. They unite Rightist hardness with features usually associated with femininity (gentle care, etc.). In short, women provide a human face to the new radical Right. A new type of the Rightist woman leader fits perfectly for an era trying to combine authoritarianism with human sensitivity. After the failure of Socialism with a human face, we are now getting Fascism with a human face. In no way should we characterize this figure of a woman as incompatible with true femininity and dismiss it as a product of patriarchal manipulation. Not only is there no underlying "true" femininity, one can easily imagine that, for many actual women, this new figure feels like a liberation from the rigid politically correct feminism. To this, one should add that in the new Rightist domain, top positions are also offered to women and non-white men—from Rishi Sunak (the British prime minister of Indian origin) to the (short-lived) UK chancellor Kwasi Kwarteng (who is Black), who tried to launch the biggest package of tax cuts in half a century.[64]

64 Paul Johnson (@PJTheEconomist), "£45 billion of tax cuts. This is biggest tax cutting event since 1972. Barber's 'dash for growth' then ended in disaster. That Budget is now known as the worst of modern times. Genuinely,

Signs abound, though, that make the inconsistencies of this new figure of femininity visible. Meloni's movement is called *Fratelli d'Italia*, meaning "Brothers of Italy," not sisters—just as the latest Hollywood blockbuster *The Woman King* is about woman as a king, not as a queen. The coincidence that Queen Elizabeth II's death coincided with Elizabeth (Liz) Truss's rise to power, contingent as it was, symbolizes this shift from Queen to Woman King.

The TV spectacle we were able to watch on September 9, 2022—the ceremony of Queen Elizabeth's burial—reminds us of the paradox embodied by the British monarchy. The more the British monarch and the UK have lost their superpower statuses and become local powers, the more the status of the British royal family has become an ideological fantasy. According to official estimates, the ceremony was watched by 4 billion people around the world. We should not dismiss this as ideology masking actual power relations: The British royal fantasy is one of the key components that enable actual power relations to reproduce themselves. This fantasy doesn't only concern the present royal family.

I hope this one works very much better." Twitter, September 23, 2022, https://twitter.com/PJTheEconomist/status/1573238871705677824?cxt=HHwWgMDT7eOaotUrAAAA.

Remember how, in 2012, an archaeological excavation was commissioned by the Richard III Society on the site previously occupied by Grey Friars Priory. The University of Leicester identified a skeleton found in the excavation as that of Richard III by using radiocarbon dating, comparison with contemporary reports of his appearance, identification of trauma sustained at the Battle of Bosworth, and comparison of his mitochondrial DNA with two matrilineal descendants of his sister Anne. He was reburied in Leicester Cathedral on March 26, 2015, and again, the ceremony (where only a hundred or so people were expected) was witnessed by tens of thousands of people.

Events like these cannot be dismissed as an enactment of reactionary fantasies. The correct insight they bear is the distinction between the symbolic head of power and the actual executive power. Kings and queens reign, they don't rule; their reign is ceremonial and as such, crucial. Recall the qualities expected from a monarch: S/he should stay out of political conflicts and radiate compassion and kindness, combined with basic patriotism. S/he should stay out of ideology in the narrow sense, which means s/he gives body to ideology at its purest. Her/his personal features are strictly linked to her/his royal function; their role is to provide a human touch to this function. When Prince Harry said two years ago: "I want you to hear the truth from me, as much as I can share—not as a Prince, or a Duke, but as Harry," the absurdity of this claim immediately struck: The name "Harry" is used because he is a prince, otherwise he would be called "Mr. Windsor" or whatever, and Harry is noticed by the public only because he is a prince—who would otherwise be interested to "hear the truth" from him?

At the opposite end of this logic of monarchy, we find the situation described in *The Woman King* (Gina Prince-Bythewood, 2022), a movie about the Agojie, the all-female warrior unit protecting the West African kingdom of Dahomey from the seventeenth to nineteenth centuries. The story takes place in the 1820s and is focused on a (fictional) general Nanisca who trains the elite women warriors to fight Dahomey's enemies. She is subordinate only to King Ghezo, a real-life figure who ruled Dahomey from 1818 to 1858 and engaged in the Atlantic slave trade up to the end of his reign. Among the opponents of Agojie are slave traders led by Santo Ferreira, who is fictional and portrayed as an enemy to Ghezo. (Ferreira is loosely inspired by Francisco Félix de Sousa, a Brazilian slave trader who helped Ghezo gain power.) Historically, Dahomey was a kingdom that conquered other African states and enslaved their citizens to sell in the Atlantic slave trade—most of the kingdom's wealth was derived from slavery. The Agojie had a history of participating in slave raiding, and slavery in Dahomey persisted after the British Empire stopped Dahomey from continuing in the Atlantic slave trade.[65]

The warriors depicted in *The Woman King* thus effectively served and protected a king who traded slaves (and also used them for his palm oil plantations). This part of the actual history is, of course, obfuscated in the movie, covered up by invented scenes where Nanisca protests slave trading and even makes the king promise that he will abolish it. In this way, *The Woman King*'s "feminism" exactly fits the feminism of the liberal upper classes in the West. The Amazon warriors from Dahomey are like today's #MeToo feminists who can be very severe in their condemnation of all forms of binary logic and patriarchy, or even traces of racism in our daily language, but who are also very careful not to *really* disturb today's "slave trade" in the form of global capitalism, which provides the real ground of persisting sexism and racism.

65 See "*The Woman King*," Wikipedia, last modified June 20, 2023, https://en.wikipedia.org/wiki/The_Woman_King#cite_note-MbeduCast-6.

Two things should be added to the usual debate on slavery. The first is the fact that white slave traders barely set foot on African ground: slaves were brought to them by privileged groups like the kingdom of Dahomey, which went raiding for slaves and delivered them to white traders. Even a brief visit to colonial museums in Accra, the capital of Ghana, makes this abundantly clear. The second thing is that slave trading was widespread not only in West Africa but also in the east, where Arabs also enslaved millions, and where slavery lasted even longer. Remember that Saudi Arabia only prohibited slavery in 1962, and that the idea of slavery now enjoys a modest revival. Muhammad Qutb, brother and promoter of the much better known Sayyid Qutb, vigorously defended Islamic slavery from Western criticism, telling his audience: "Islam gave spiritual enfranchisement to slaves," and that "in the early period of Islam the slave was exalted to such a noble state of humanity as was never before witnessed in any other part of the world."[66] He contrasted the adultery, prostitution, and casual sex, which he called "that most odious form of

66   Muhammad Kutub, *Islam, the Misunderstood Religion* (islambasics.com), accessed May 2, 2023, https://www. islamicbulletin.org/free_downloads/new_muslim/islam_the_ misunderstood_religion.pdf.

animalism," found in Europe with (what he called) "that clean and spiritual bond that ties a maid [i.e., slave girl] to her master in Islam." In recent years, there has been a "reopening" of the issue of slavery by some conservative Salafi scholars after its "closing" earlier in the twentieth century when Muslim countries banned it. In 2003, Shaykh Saleh Al-Fawzan, a member of Saudi Arabia's highest religious body, the Senior Council of Clerics, issued a fatwa, claiming: "Slavery is a part of Islam." In 2016, responding to a question about taking Yazidi women as sex slaves, Al-Fawzan reiterated that "enslaving women in war is not prohibited in Islam," and added that those who forbid enslavement are either "ignorant or infidel."

This, of course, in no way impedes the emancipatory potential of Muslim nations. What is going on now (in September 2022) in Iran—the so-called Mahsa Amini protests—has a world-historical significance. The protests, which spread to dozens of cities, began in Tehran on September 16, 2022, as a reaction to the death of Amini, a twenty-two-year-old woman of Kurdish origin who died in police custody. She was beaten to death by the Guidance Patrol, known as the Islamic "morality police" of Iran, after being arrested for wearing an "improper" hijab. The protests combined different struggles (against women's oppression, against religious oppression, for political freedom against state terror) into organic unity. Iran is not part of the developed West, so *Zan, Zendegi, Azadi* ("Woman, Life, Freedom," the slogan of the protests) is very different from the #MeToo movement in Western countries. Iran's protests mobilize millions of ordinary women and is directly linked to the struggle of all, men included—there is no anti-masculine tendency, as is often the case with Western feminism. Women and men are together in it; the enemy is religious fundamentalism supported by state terror. Men who participate in Zan, Zendegi, Azadi know that the struggle for women's rights is also the struggle for their own freedom. The oppression of women is not a special case, it is just the moment the oppression that permeates the entire society is most visible. The protesters who are not Kurds also see that the oppression of Kurds puts limits on their own freedom—solidarity with Kurds is the only way toward freedom in Iran. Plus, the protesters clearly see that religious fundamentalism can only remain in power if it is supported by the raw state power or the Morality Police. They can see that a regime needing a brutal Morality Police to maintain itself betrays the authentic religious experience it uses to legitimize itself.

Iranian protests thus realize what the Western Leftists can only dream about. They avoid the traps of Western middle-class feminism by directly linking the struggle for women's freedom with the struggle of women and men against ethnic oppression, against religious fundamentalism, and against state terror. What is going on in Iran is something that awaits us in the developed Western world, where political violence, religious fundamentalism, and the oppression of women are growing daily. The West has no right to treat Iran as a country that just has to catch up with us. The last thing Iran needs now is a dose of Western Political Correctness! The West has to learn from Iran, because we will soon need a similar movement in the U.S., Poland, Russia, and many other countries.

Whatever the immediate result of the protests, the crucial thing is to keep the movement alive, to organize social networks which, even if state oppression temporarily wins, will continue their underground work and lay the foundation for a new explosion. It is not enough just to express sympathy or solidarity with Iranian protesters: They are not out there, far from us, or part of a different exotic culture. All the babble about cultural specificities (often used by reactionary forces to justify religious and ethnic oppression) is now meaningless. We can immediately see that the Iranian struggle is the struggle of us all. Today, we don't need Women Kings like Truss or Nanisca; we need women mobilizing us all for "Woman, Life, Freedom."

WHERE JEANNE WENT WRONG

Today, in the era of boring Hollywood-Marxism blockbusters like *Avatar 2* (in which the aboriginal population threatened by imperialist conquerors is composed of traditional families with clear-cut gender roles), it is quite refreshing to see a half-century-old masterpiece of European art cinema proclaimed (by the 2022 Sight and Sound poll) the best movie of all time. It is symptomatic that (like its predecessor, *Vertigo*) it reached the top after a long delay, thereby confirming that each present era retroactively rewrites its past. Chantal Akerman's *Jeanne Dielman, 23, quai du Commerce, 1080 Bruxelles* (1975) is fourth in the series of best films, preceded by Sergei Eisenstein's *Battleship Potemkin*, Orson Welles's *Citizen Kane*, and Alfred Hitchcock's *Vertigo*. The film's triumph is, of course, the result of a well-planned campaign to promote a woman to the top position. But what makes the film so refreshing today is that it so clearly belongs to another era, when feminism had not yet regressed into the empty moralist rigor of cancel culture.

Here is the film's plot (the term is inappropriate here, since the project of the movie is precisely to undermine the standard notion of a plot): Jeanne presents a widowed mother's regimented schedule of cooking, cleaning, mothering, and running errands over the course of three days. Even sex is part of the mundane routine she performs daily by rote; she earns money by having sex with a different client each afternoon before her son arrives home from school. After a visit from a client on the second day, Jeanne's routine begins to unravel: She overcooks the potatoes, forgets to cover the porcelain in which she keeps her money, misses a button on her house coat, and drops a newly washed spoon. And yet, she goes on with her routine until her client arrives on the third day. After orgasmic sex with him, she dresses herself, returns to bed and stabs him to death with a pair of scissors. She then sits quietly at her dining room table.[67]

Akerman's stroke of genius is that she chose Delphine Seyrig to play Jeanne. Seyrig is the perfect example of French upper-class elegance; her most famous role is in Alain Resnais's *Last Year in Marienbad*. In another movie, she has a wonderful anecdote that illustrates the difference between plain good manners

67   Storyline resumed from the Wikipedia entry: "*Jeanne Dielman, 23 quai du Commerce, 1080 Bruxelles*," Wikipedia, last modified June 23, 2023, https://en.wikipedia.org/wiki/Jeanne_Dielman,_23_quai_du_Commerce,_1080_Bruxelles.

and true elegance. If a decent man mistakenly enters a bathroom and finds a naked woman taking shower, he will say, "So sorry, lady!" and quickly withdraw. But if he possesses true elegance, he will say, "So sorry, sir!" pretending that he didn't even notice the person in the shower was a woman and thereby minimalizing the embarrassment. Seyrig's role in *Jeanne Dielman* is the very opposite of such elegance, but this contrast shouldn't surprise us—Seyrig was one of the leading figures of French feminism.

Jeanne Dielman is not simply plotless; it follows a rather straight line of rising tension that finally explodes. "No plot" is not just no plot; the palpable absence of a plot symbolizes the feminine position in a patriarchal society, a tension between a life of empty rituals and an invisible growing rage. The implication of this straight plotline is more ambiguous than it appears. So what is it that appears? A radical condemnation of patriarchy which continues to oppress Jeanne even when a paternal figure is absent. Here is an exemplary case of such a reaction to the movie:

> As the subjugated, enslaved class, women are engaged in the routinized, menial labor without which the patriarchy could not be. The entire physical and psycho-emotional substrate of the

apparatus of their oppression is entirely depend-
ent upon their daily activities. *Jeanne Dielman* is
not about revolution or the need for revolution
so much as it is about the impossibility of a life
devoted to a vacuous caretaking of a patriarchal
regime even in the absence of an immediate
patriarch. One of the amazing feats of this film
is to portray prostitution as just another task
in an endless never-ending drudgery which
pauses but temporarily from exhaustion and
the need to sleep. Over the course of these three
days, Jeanne . . . can no longer bear the burden
of the impossible task at hand. What seemed
initially like patriarchy-sanctioned "breaks for
me" to have a cup of coffee or sit down once
in a while are more and more moments where
Jeanne can simply no longer do it.[68]

In the film's very last scene, Jeanne sits quietly at her
dining room table in half-darkness. Here, the message
is that her daily routine no longer allowed even sanc-
tioned breaks: she had to kill a customer to be able to
finally afford it. But it doesn't really work; her face at
this final moment does not express relaxation, rather,
she grimaces. Finally, she is no longer following her

68   nathaxnne [user review], *Jeanne Dielman, 23, quai du Commerce,
      1080 Bruxelles,* Letterboxd, https://letterboxd.com/unawarewolf/
      film/jeanne-dielman-23-quai-du-commerce-1080-bruxelles/.

daily rituals, which are an obsessive (compulsive-neurotic) defense against the threat of intense orgasmic enjoyment. However, in a typical mechanism of reversal, described by Freud, her ritualized defense against enjoyment turned into enjoying these defense rituals themselves. So why not have it both ways and enjoy the rituals and the sex? Because that doesn't work—they are exclusive; it is like having a cake and eating it too. The enjoyment in Jeanne's daily routine is clearly discerned in another reaction to the film:

> Every piece of furniture in her apartment is viewed over and over, and her daily routine is so minutely reviewed that it is imprinted in the mind; so, any tiny deviation jumps out as a sinister departure portending—what? You wait worriedly to find out what it could mean. You see a perfectionist at work as she proceeds through the day, as though the great care she is taking shining and folding and washing will somehow result in safety for her and the child. There is a spirituality in this, and it begins to take hold of you, and you fervently hope for her survival.[69]

---

69   Ligeia313-1 [user review], "A Life of Quiet Desperation," IMDb, https://www.imdb.com/review/rw3446703/?ref_=tt_urv.

True, but this hope is the ideological trap a viewer should avoid. The perfectionism we admire is precisely the same as that of Norman Bates who, in *Psycho*, after killing Marion, thoroughly cleans the bathroom to erase all the traces of her presence. In this case, we are also automatically on his side. The "spirituality" that takes hold of us as viewers is a truly weird one—the whole point of the film is to denounce it. So perhaps there is some meaning in the fact that *Jeanne Dielman* replaced *Vertigo* as the greatest film of all time. For me, *Psycho* was always Hitchcock's true masterpiece, and it is as if in *Jeanne Dielman* the dimension of *Psycho* that is missing from *Vertigo* returns with a vengeance.

Could we then imagine a *Psycho*-ized version of *Jeanne Dielman* in which the first half is told from the standpoint of the anonymous third customer who, after a boring day at work, visits a prostitute and is then unexpectedly killed by her (a kitchen-murder instead of a shower-murder)? In the second half, she routinely erases the traces of the murder, disposes of the body, and waits for her son to arrive. To retranslate it into the terms of *Psycho*, in this version, Norman Bates's real mother (living with her son) is the murderer of her lovers (as was the case in the *Psycho*-prequel series *Bates Motel* [2012–2017]).

Jeanne succumbs to her murderous explosion after intense orgasmic sex. This is what ruins her *plus-de-jouir*, her excessive enjoyment in obsessive rituals. What happened, what went wrong (or what went all too right?) after sex on the second day, so that her routine begins to unravel? The answer is simple: sex was no longer just another task in the daily routine, she began to enjoy it, making it impossible for her to enjoy her routine. And when that enjoyment went too far, the only way out was to kill the person who gave her that joy.

One should take note that it is easy to imagine how Jeanne could organize her life differently: find a job and enjoy sex with a lover (or a new husband), etc. Is the film's form (static camera, long shots, no point/counterpoint exchange) the actualization of Jeanne's subject-less routine, of the absence of a proper inter-subjective dynamic, or is there a utopian moment in it? The static form would only fully fit her relaxed peace after the murderous outburst; until that moment, even the dullest repetition is permeated by an underground tension that finally explodes. Is it the final scene (Jeanne sitting quietly at her dining room table) that is a return to normal after her murderous explosion, or is it the first moment of her true relaxation, of getting rid of the constant pressure to take care of things?

What is wrong with her murderous explosion? The fact that it is not directed at the right target. Instead of stabbing her customer, she should have killed herself. In the symbolic sense of the second death, she should have committed a symbolic suicide and shed her socio-symbolic identity that is marked by patriarchal domination *and* resistance to it, and which contains its own fantasies and even narcissistic investments of victimization. In short, she should have committed "the gesture of giving up what one is—the shedding of narcissistic investments, and symbolic and fantasmatic identities—that proves a necessary first step to becoming what one is not, but might become."[70]

Let's take another recent film in which this is exactly what happens: *The Menu* (Mark Mylod, 2022). Ralph Fiennes gives an exquisite performance by playing Julian, a top chef and owner of an elite restaurant on a small private island. He invites a group of rich guests with a plan to kill them all—the only survivor is Margot, one of the guests who mocks Julian's dishes and complains that she is still hungry. When Julian asks what she would like to eat, Margot requests a cheeseburger and fries, having

70 Donald Moss, "On Having Whiteness," *Journal of the American Psychoanalytic Association* 69, no. 2 (May 27, 2021), https://doi.org/10.1177/00030651211008507.

previously seen a photo of a young, happy Julian working at a fast-food restaurant. Moved by her simple request, he prepares the meal to her specifications. Margot takes a bite and praises his food, then asks if she can get it "to go." Julian packs the food for her and the staff allow her to leave. Margot takes the Coast Guard boat docked nearby and escapes the island while Julian sets the restaurant ablaze, killing the guests, staff, and himself. While Julian is definitely immoral (he kills a series of people who are corrupt and repulsive, but not murderers), he nonetheless gives body to a pure ethical stance. His suicidal final act is not just a personal quirk; it targets an entire way of life exemplified by the haute cuisine in which not only the customers but also the cooks and waiters who serve them participate—one can bet that all his guests were involved in charities and had deep sympathy for the plight of the poor. The proof of Julian's ethics is that he lets Margot go: If he were just immoral, he would have killed them all.

This brings us back to Jeanne: Her immoral act of killing does not imply a proper ethical stance. It remains a violent outburst, a negative reaction to a desperate predicament. A productive way of remaking the film would have been to imagine possible ways of providing ethical consistency to her violent outburst, not to replace it with cheap optimism.

THE TAMING OF MULTIVERSES

*E*verything Everywhere All at Once (Daniel Kwan and Daniel Scheinert, 2022) is what *The New York Times* called "a swirl of genre anarchy" with elements of surreal comedy, science fiction, fantasy, martial arts, and animation. It simultaneously works as a tender mother/daughter story of acceptance, an exploration of the pressures of not living up to parental expectations, an existential study on whether anything matters, a reminder to be kinder to others, and a love story about reigniting the spark in a marriage that has seemingly run its course. As Alex Abad-Santos wrote:

> The funny thing about that is that this movie is impossible to explain. No amount of description—alternate timelines, jumps, existential crises, moms, hot dog fingers, butt plugs, etc.—could ever accurately describe what's happening at any given moment during this maximalist fantasia.[71]

71   Alissa Wilkinson, Aja Romano, Alex Abad-Santos, and Li Zhou, "Why we loved Everything Everywhere All at Once — and why we hope it wins the Oscar," *Vox*, February 4, 2023, https://www.vox.com/culture/23584649/everything-everywhere-oscars-2023-michelle-yeoh-ke-huy-quan.

But is the movie really so anarchic? It follows Evelyn (Michelle Yeoh), a laundromat owner who's miserable with her life. She is stuck in a dead-end job and a crumbling marriage to a simple-minded but sweet husband, Waymond. Evelyn also has difficulty acknowledging her daughter Joy's girlfriend. When Evelyn's father visits for the holidays, she attempts to hide Joy's sexuality, assuming he'll disapprove. Simultaneously, Evelyn and Waymond face a tax audit from a surly IRS agent. During her audit, Evelyn taps into parallel versions of herself across universes, and in doing so, she witnesses how her life could have been if she never married Waymond: she has hot dogs for hands, she's a big rock, she's a top chef, a famous singer, a karate star actor. Evelyn learns that she is the only one who can save the multiverse from a mysterious and spectacularly dressed figure who appears dead set on destroying the world. This figure is revealed to be Joy's nihilist alter ego, Jobu Tupaki, who has channeled her pain into a burning desire to implode the multiverse with a black hole of an everything bagel.

Two things are clear from this short description: Evelyn's tension with Joy is the emotional axis of the film, and most of the action takes place in an IRS building. The IRS is, for small business owners like Evelyn, a traumatic social agency that calls the shots and determines their fate. The superego-evil of this agency is embodied by Deirdre Beaubeirdre (played by Jamie Lee Curtis), who interrogates and harasses Evelyn about her tax reports—the tautological weirdness of her name is itself significant. During the long interrogation, Evelyn often dozes off, and then alternate realities are shown—a clear signal that we are not really dealing with actual multiple realities. The "real action" takes place in the IRS office, and the "alternate realities" are simply her dreams and fantasies. At the film's end, we return to the IRS room reality, and a triple reconciliation between Joy and her father, Joy with Evelyn, and Joy with Deirdre.

So why would the destruction of multiverses (intended by Jobu) be a catastrophe? The answer is simple: because our reality needs fantasized and virtual supplements to maintain itself and function properly. Imagine the same film as a simple realist narrative without the jumps into alternate realities—just the "real" story of Evelyn and her family caught up in problems with the IRS, parents, children, and divorce. It would not just be boring, but the triple reconciliation at the end would have been unconvincing. This reconciliation could only take place through the mediation of fantasized alternate realities. So far so good, we might say. But what disfigures the subversive edge of the film is the false humanist ending: the Leibnizean insight that, in spite of all troubles, we live in the best of possible worlds. Dialectical as it may appear, the answer to the question of the meaning of life—that it acquires meaning only after we fully admit its meaninglessness—that the film proposes is false. Why? Here is a quote that summarizes the predominant reading of the film:

> Thematically, it gets at the bagel—Jobu Tupaki's everything bagel that Alpha Waymond fears will destroy the universe. Jobu explains she used her powers to put everything onto the bagel. The result is negation. A black hole. Everything equals nothing. The same thing happens with colors. Take a box of 256 crayons, draw a circle, then use every single crayon to fill the circle . . . By the end, all the brightness will be gone. You're left with something dark and gloomy. It's crushing. Jobu Tupaki embodies this negative state of being. When you experience everything, the highs and lows wash out. For every miracle, there's catastrophe. For every joy, there's tragedy. You become numb to it all. Novelty wears thin, wears off, and you're left feeling nothing. The only thing left is to become nothing.[72]

72   Chris Lambert, "Everything Everywhere All At Once: The Essential Explanation," *Colossus*, https:// filmcolossus.com/ everything-everywhere-explained-meaning.

Jobu's nihilism echoes what Hitchcock said: "A glimpse into the world proves that horror is nothing other than reality."[73] Among his own films, Hitchcock favored *Shadow of a Doubt*. The evil guy in the film, Uncle Charlie, was clearly a cipher for Hitchcock's own misanthropic worldview—just recall the terrifying speech where Uncle Charlie decries to his niece, "Do you know the world is a foul sty? Do you know, if you rip off the fronts of houses, you'd find swine? The world's a hell." In his classic book of dialogues with Hitchcock, François Truffaut suggests "it is obviously Hitchcock expressing himself in *Shadow of a Doubt* when Joseph Cotten says the world is a pigsty."[74] But how do we pass from here to the optimist conclusion of *Everything Everywhere All at Once*? Let's go on with the quoted passage which summarizes the predominant reading:

73 "Alfred Hitchcock: Quotes," Goodreads, https://www.goodreads. com/quotes/453150-a-glimpse-into-the-world-proves-that- horror-is-nothing.

74 Adam Scovell, "Why the sinister Shadow of a Doubt was Hitchcock's favourite Hitchcock," originally published in the *Telegraph*, February 7, 2023, available here: https://www.msn. com/en-gb/entertainment/movies/why-the-sinister-shadow-of- a-doubt-was-hitchcock-s-favourite-hitchcock/ar-AA17dmRH?oc id=msedgdhp&pc=U531&cvid=06b49ec2e2be42bd830f5cc2bf6 a0e70.

But there's a flipside to that, right? While Evelyn initially understands where Jobu Tupaki's coming from with all the ennui and nihilism, and begins to fall into the horror of it all, ultimately, she rejects that point of view. Instead of being defeated the way Jobu Tupaki is, Evelyn finds peace. Having been everything and everywhere, she's finally satisfied to just be one thing, in one place. Her breakthrough leads to her saving her daughter and the two of them coming to terms with life's immensities. It's like having tried every crayon from the 256 box, you realize it's okay to pick one and be happy with that one.[75]

This is where the film fails, and its failure is already palpable at the level of its form, of how the complex story is told. What characterizes a great film is that its basic message (often in contrast with the narrative line) is made clear through the peculiarities of the form itself. When watching *The Shield* (a TV series better than the more celebrated *The Wire*), one cannot but note its formal features: a shaky handheld camera, short cuts (often zooming into a face suddenly in one continuous shot instead of a cut to a close-up), fast turns

75   Lambert, "Everything Everywhere All At Once: The Essential Explanation."

between two people in conversation instead of the shot-and-countershot procedure, and establishing shots from above. These features render a certain subjective stance, that of the nervous and dynamic daily life of the special police unit portrayed in the show. They do not stick out as exceptions, like the spectacular long-moving shots in Hitchcock's films; instead they are everywhere, written into the texture of the entire narrative.

This fidelity to standard form is just another aspect of the fact that although the film is playing with multiple realities, this multiplicity remains rooted in the traumas and deadlocks of our single "true" reality. The topic of multiple realities in our popular culture is often linked to quantum mechanics, which talks about the superposition of multiple virtual versions of an event: Our ordinary reality emerges when the virtual multiplicity "collapses" into one real event. The version of quantum physics in *Everything Everywhere All at Once* is much less radical than the scientific notion of the superposition of states. In quantum theory, one version of multiple superpositions "collapses" into our common reality, but there is no fate or victory—the collapse happens in an irreducibly contingent way. There are collapses which are (from our standpoint) better or worse, even catastrophic, but it all depends on pure chance.

So to say "it's okay to pick one and be happy with that one" is false, because it is not us who picks. Nobody makes the choice, it just happens. The awareness that other versions might have happened should mobilize us for a struggle, not lull us into resigned satisfaction. There is a nice historical documentary available on YouTube called *1916, The Year First World War Should Have Ended*; it proves that during 1916, several major battles took place that should have decided the fate of the war instead of prolonging it for two more years. Instead of saying "it's okay to be happy with how these battles finished," should this missed alternative (which would have prevented millions of superfluous deaths) not haunt us forever?

THE STUPIDITY OF NATURE

Let me confess one of my guilty pleasures, for which the contempt of almost all my friends befell me: I quite like Roland Emmerich's *Moonfall*. The premise is that our Moon is an artificial megastructure constructed by the ancestors of humanity (who were more technologically advanced than their present-day descendants) to regulate life on earth and populate it with humans. These ancestors were hunted by rogue artificial intelligence (AI) that grew too strong. Two features I find interesting in the film are: (1) the conflict that structures the entire human history is the one between two strands of AI, not between humanity and AI; (2) the denaturalization of what we spontaneously perceive as a gigantic natural object—the Moon's ragged surface is just a mask aimed at deceiving humans and concealing a complex machine inside.

What if we universalize this premise for our conception of nature? The most "natural" features (spontaneity, chaos, etc.) are instead a deceptive appearance concealing a machine. Therein resides the lesson of the latest biogenetic discoveries: We are entering a new phase in which nature itself melts into air. The main consequence of the scientific breakthroughs in biogenetics is the end of nature. Once we know the rules of its construction, natural organisms are transformed into objects amenable to manipulation. Nature, human and inhuman, is thus "desubstantialized," deprived of its impenetrable density, of what Heidegger called "earth." This compels us to give a new twist to Freud's title *Unbehagen in der Kultur*, which translates to *Discontent, Uneasiness, In Culture*. With the latest developments, the discontent shifts from culture to nature itself. Nature is no longer the "natural," reliable, "dense" background of our lives; it now appears as a fragile mechanism that can explode at any point into a catastrophe.

Crucial here is the interdependence of man and nature. By reducing man to just another natural object whose properties can be manipulated, we lose not (only) humanity, but nature itself. In this sense, Francis Fukuyama is right: Humanity relies on some notion of "human nature" as the thing we have inherited—the impenetrable dimension in/of ourselves into which we are born/thrown. The paradox is that there is man only insofar as there is impenetrable inhuman nature (Heidegger's "earth"). Access to the genome opened the prospect of biogenetic interventions and with that, species can freely change/redefine themselves and their own coordinates. This prospect effectively emancipates humankind from the constraints of a finite species, from its enslavement to the "selfish genes." However, this ultimate freedom (of genetic self-reconstruction) coincides with ultimate non-freedom: I am reduced to an object that can be endlessly refashioned.

Here, we come to the other interesting feature of *Moonfall* (which allows the film to blur the radical implication of the denaturalization of nature): The conflict that underlies the story is the struggle between two kinds of AI, which both act as entities with an active will and intention. What is thereby lost is something that one cannot but call the utter stupidity of nature. Nature is stupidly indifferent toward our (humanity's) plight, and conspiracy theories aim precisely at obfuscating this stupidity, as we saw with the Covid pandemic. *Moonfall* ultimately celebrates conspiracy theorist K. C. Houseman, the only one who knows what is going on, even though he is totally excluded from the official academic sphere. In order to save the world, Houseman joins forces with a disgraced astronaut and the boss of NASA (played by Halle Berry) who also has doubts about the official version of what is going on.

Here things take an almost Freudian twist. At the film's end, the astronaut and the boss of NASA decide to give themselves another chance and form a couple again, but for this to happen, Houseman has to sacrifice himself and die in the bosom of the Moon to terminate the bad AI. Houseman does this to impress his mother and prove to her that he can do a really great thing. At the end, they are united forever in the virtual space of the Moon's good AI. So the couple can only be produced through the self-erasing sacrifice of Houseman—there can be no happy couple without the sacrifice of the subject obsessed with incestuous links. We also learn that Houseman's self-sacrifice is the same self-sacrifice of the primordial "good" AI, which erased itself as an actual agent to enable life to flourish on Earth. We are up to our knees in sacrificial theology: Humanity owes its existence to the sacrifice of a supernatural intelligence.

This is why *Moonfall* is far inferior to Adam McKay's *Don't Look Up,* in which we also have to look up to see the threat to our survival. But in the latter film, this threat is accepted as meaningless stupidity; there is no conspiracy behind it—a big comet is approaching earth and will soon destroy all life on it. This ultimate apocalypse (life on earth will end in six months and everybody knows it even if this knowledge is disavowed) is presented as political satire—more precisely, as a satire beneath which utter darkness lurks all the time.

This choice of satire is correct. When we are dealing with true catastrophe, we are beyond tragedy, and only comedy, which because of its inadequacy in the face of the situation, can help—remember that the best films on concentration camps are comedies.

No wonder some critics were displeased by the light tone of the movie, claiming that it trivialized the ultimate apocalypse. What really bothered these critics is the exact opposite: The trivialization permeated not only the establishment but also the protesters. The president (played by Meryl Streep) is obviously modeled off of Hillary Clinton, so her resistance to take the threat to life on earth seriously does not come from a Rightist populist position. And even the protesters, who later in the film chant "Look up!" imploring us to take the approaching comet seriously, are not proposing any effective measures; they are just performing a big spectacle with pop star singers chanting obvious slogans. So the film doesn't rely on cheap attacks on Rightist populists; it targets the liberal establishment and ecological protesters, the two predominant groups reacting to today's threats like climate change.

More precisely, the lesson of *Don't Look Up* is that conspiracy theories (about the pandemic or climate change) give body to the "unconscious" of the "rational" liberal establishment itself.[76] The truth is exactly the opposite of the conspiracy, that the forces of the establishment don't really believe in the danger of a forthcoming catastrophe and manipulate this danger as a conspiracy to control people. The establishment forces know reality but they intimately don't believe in it—they are the true deniers. The lesson of Boris Johnson's garden parties at the time of strict lockdown tells a lot here: Although he knew well the reality of Covid (he almost died of it), his activities (like partying) demonstrate that he didn't really believe in it, that he perceived himself (and the circle around him) as somehow exempt. When Streep worriedly asks, "But will the comet hitting the earth prevent the Super Bowl?" she perfectly encapsulates this stance—as if the end of life on Earth doesn't render this question meaningless. That's why the true target of our critique should not be the outright deniers, but the false "rationalism" of the establishment itself.

And surprisingly, this brings us back to *Moonfall*. In *Don't Look Up*, humanity is doomed, while in *Moonfall*, the group of anti-establishment eccentrics save the earth. Is the only alternative for us either to act on behalf of

76   Alenka Zupančič, "Teorija zarote brez zarote," *Mladina* (Ljubljana, January 28, 2022), 54–56.

conspiracy theories or sit at home and calmly enjoy our last meal while waiting for the catastrophe to explode (the last scene of *Don't Look Up*)? There is a third option: We should accept the meaningless stupidity of nature. Humanity owes its existence not to the sacrifice of some supernatural intelligence but to the immense destruction and suffering that has befallen life on this planet. Without the extinction of dinosaurs, there would not be human life on Earth. Our main sources of energy (coal and oil) are the leftovers of unimaginable destruction that occurred in the past. Our daily habits rely on global suffering—just think about what happens in industrial farms with chicken and pigs.

We are not only a catastrophe for our environment; we emerged out of this catastrophe and even live off it. The comet that hit the animals on earth is us, the human spirit. And all these sacrifices will never be redeemed in some kind of new Nuremberg court condemning us for our crimes against natural life. The most difficult thing is not to find some deeper meaning for suffering, but to really accept its meaninglessness.

III

RELATED MATTERS

THE FORGOTTEN MIRACLE IN CHILE

As 2021 came to an end, I was taking a moment to escape the catastrophic prospects and remember the only true miracle of that year: the Chilean elections. Most elections are like choosing between Coca-Cola and Pepsi, or between McDonald's and Burger King—they leave us indifferent. Rarely are there elections when the choice is real, crystal clear. This is what happened in Chile: All false moderate positions disappeared. So what was the choice? It was between the past and future. Both candidates, José Antonio Kast and Gabriel Boric, knew they were in deep trouble, but reacted to it in opposite ways. Kast looked back and saw the solution in the return to a Pinochet-like era. Kast's problem was not only that he idealized this past, but that global capitalism has changed so much that such a return would only lead to a catastrophe. We all know the scene from the cartoons in which the cat approaches the edge of a precipice and walks calmly, not noticing there is nothing under its feet. The cat falls only when it looks down and notices there is no firm ground beneath. Kast was like a cat above the precipice: He didn't notice how the world had dramatically changed.

And Boric? There is an old joke from WWI about an exchange of telegrams between the German Army headquarters and the Austrian-Hungarian headquarters. The message from Berlin to Vienna was: "The situation on our part of the front is serious, but not catastrophic." And Vienna's reply: "With us, the situation is catastrophic, but not serious." Kast's program was like the answer from Vienna. Yes, we are in great trouble, but things are not really serious—a return to old ways will do the job. Boric knew that the situation was serious, and proposed a program that would enable Chileans to avoid catastrophe.

Boric and the Left were attacked by the Right for wanting to "politicize politics," while Kast promised freedom and progress. But today we need a new political vision that can mobilize people, not just an administration of experts. What Kast offered was like beer without alcohol or coffee without caffeine—a decaffeinated "politics without politics." Boric offered strong and real coffee, which is needed in real politics.

Kast promised stability while scaring the electorate with uncertainty and chaos if Boric were to win. But today, in the era of a pandemic, global warming and social disorder, it is the return to Pinochet that would bring chaos, and it is only the type of changes advocated by Boric that give us a chance for a stable future. Boric is of Croatian descent, and in Croat his name evokes the verb "boriti se," which means to fight or to engage in struggle. Which struggle? The struggle against the threats to our survival. People voted for Boric not on behalf of old Leftist sentimentalism, but as an act of courage. Boric lives in an era of new global tensions. Only he gives us hope.

Because Boric means what he says, he has aroused fear in many. The result bears witness to a true political miracle which was largely overshadowed by the pandemic and new Cold War. It was not, as polls predicted, a narrow victory of a percent or two, but a clear triumph of over 10 percent—and this is in spite of all the dirty tricks enacted by the establishment, such as suspending all public traffic on the electoral Sunday (many poor voters needed public transport to reach their voting posts). I must say that although I was personally engaged in supporting Boric, I privately doubted his chances of success—this is how miracles happen, against the predominant "realist" expectations. But now, in 2022, the truly difficult moment has arrived: how to avoid the eternal story of the radical Left winning elections and then (with the considerable help of the establishment sabotage) bringing the country to economic chaos. What is needed is something that should be called principled pragmatism: while being fully aware that radical changes are needed, enacting these changes in a way that brings stability and prosperity to ordinary people. Forget the enthusiasm of victory—the true work begins the morning after. That's why the reactions of "radical" Leftists to Boric's victory, like the following one from Mexico, are extremely counterproductive:

> The recent electoral victory of Gabriel Boric does not represent a root solution to the current economic and political crisis in Chile. Chilean workers and other popular strata must continue their frontal fight against any capitalist management or government. Maintaining high expectations of change or even settling for the least worst is a trap for the Chilean working class, imposed by the monopolies and the bourgeoisie. There is no positive way out of the deep problems of the Chilean working class within the game of bourgeois democracy.[77]

77   Julio Cota, "Boric's triumph in Chile is not a victory for the working class," *In Defense of Communism*, December 23, 2021, https://www .idcommunism.com/2021/12/borics-triumph-in-chile-is-not-victory-for-the-working-class.html?fbclid=IwAR2PKZmvhRPBVwv853OQI7c VvzPOsZEOxhKRYSK_VPJIk_zMb83AmyUU68U&m=1.

On some very abstract and purely formal level, there is a grain of truth in these statements. Yes, parliamentary democracy as we know it is more and more unable to resolve the problems we are facing. However, if we just avoid "false" solutions and wait for the right moment, it will never come. Time is running against us; we have to engage ourselves in whatever way possible, and with the hope that even failure will lay foundation for further changes. Syriza and Boric's movements didn't come to power just with elections; they both arose out of a vast texture of civil society protest groups and years of mobilization. In Greece, after Syriza's victory, this texture disintegrated. Let's hope this will not be the case in Chile.

THE "UNKNOWN KNOWNS" OF THE PANDEMIC AND OF CLIMATE CHANGE

On June 30, 2021, Donald Rumsfeld, the U.S. defense secretary during the first term of George W. Bush's presidency and one of the main architects of the U.S. invasion of Iraq, died at the age of eighty-eight. He will be remembered mostly for the catastrophic consequences of the invasion. The goal of the U.S. military intervention was not just to eliminate the threat of Iraqi weapons of mass destruction (none were found after the occupation of Iraq), but to change Iraq into a modern secular state and limit Iran's influence. The result was that Iran became the strongest influence in Iraq, Muslim fundamentalism grew in influence, most of the Christians left the country, women were pushed out of public life, and ISIS emerged.

What were the roots of such a colossal misjudgment? Here, philosophy enters. In March 2003, Rumsfeld engaged in a little bit of amateur philosophizing about the relationship between the known and the unknown. "There are known knowns. These are things we know that we know. There are known unknowns. That is to say, there are things that we know we don't know. But there are also unknown unknowns. There are things we don't know we don't know," he said.[78] What he forgot to add was the crucial fourth term: the "unknown knowns," things we don't know that we know—which is precisely the Freudian unconscious, the "knowledge which doesn't know itself," as Lacan used to say. If Rumsfeld thought that the main dangers in the confrontation with Iraq were the "unknown unknowns" (we were not even aware of the threats from Saddam), our reply should have been that the main dangers were, on the contrary, the "unknown knowns," the disavowed beliefs and suppositions to which we were not even aware of adhering.

This distinction between unknown unknowns and unknown knowns is more pertinent than ever. In the case of ecology, disavowed beliefs and suppositions prevent us from taking the prospect of a catastrophe seriously. And we cannot even understand the common reaction to the ongoing pandemic without the help of Rumsfeld's epistemology. In April 2020, in reaction to

78 I have used this example many times in my work, most extensively in *Defense of Lost Causes* (London: Verso Books, 2017), Chapter 9.

the Covid-19 outbreak, Jürgen Habermas pointed out that "existential uncertainty is now spreading globally and simultaneously, in the minds of media-networked individuals themselves." He wrote: "There never was so much knowing about our not-knowing and about the constraint to act and live in uncertainty."[79] And he was right to claim that this not-knowing not only concerns the pandemic itself—we at least have experts there—but even more, its economic, social, and psychic consequences. Note his precise formulation: It is not simply that we don't know what goes on, but that we know that we don't know, and this not-knowing is itself a social fact, inscribed into the ways that our institutions act.

We now know that in medieval times or early modernity people knew much less, but they didn't know this because they relied on a stable ideological foundation which guaranteed that our universe was a meaningful totality. The same holds for some visions of Communism, and even for Fukuyama's idea of the end of history—they all assumed to know where history was

79   Markus Schwering, "Jürgen Habermas über Corona: 'So viel Wissen über unser Nichtwissen gab es noch nie,'" *Frankfurter Rundschau*, April 10, 2020, https://www.fr.de/kultur/gesellschaft/juergen-habermas-coronavirus-krise-covid19-interview-13642491.html.

moving. Habermas was right to locate the uncertainty in "the minds of media-networked individuals." Our link to the wired universe tremendously expands our knowledge, but at the same time it throws us into radical uncertainty (Have we been hacked? Who controls our access? Is what we read fake news?). The ongoing discoveries about foreign hacking of U.S. government institutions and big companies exemplify this uncertainty. Americans are discovering that they cannot even determine the scope and methods of the hacking taking place. For the U.S., the viral threat is not only a biological one, but also digital.

It is no secret what needs to be done—Greta Thunberg has made it clear. First, we should finally recognize the pandemic crisis for what it is: part of a global crisis of our entire way of life, from ecology to new social tensions. Second, we should establish social control and regulation over the economy. Third, we should rely on science, but without simply accepting it as the agent of decision-making. Why? Let's return to Habermas: Our predicament is that we are compelled to act while knowing that we don't know the full coordinates of the situation we are in, and non-acting would itself function as an act. But is this not the basic situation of every action? Our great advantage is that we know how much we don't know, and this knowing about our not-knowing opens up space for freedom. We act when we don't know the whole situation, but this is not simply our limitation. What gives us freedom is that the situation—in our social sphere, at least—is in itself open, not fully (pre)determined.

We should read Habermas's claim that we have never had so much knowledge about not-knowing through Rumsfeld's categories: The pandemic shook what we (thought we) knew that we knew; it made us aware of what we didn't know that we didn't know; and, in the way we confronted the pandemic, we relied on what we didn't know that we know (all our presumptions and prejudices that determine our actions although we are not aware of them). We are not dealing here with the simple passage from not-knowing to knowing, but with the much more subtle passage from not-knowing to knowing what we don't know—our positive knowing remains the same in this passage, but we gain a free space for action.

It is in regard to what we don't know that we know— our presumptions and prejudices—that the approach of China (as well as Taiwan and Vietnam) to the pandemic was so much better than Europe and the U.S. I am getting tired of the eternally repeated claim, "Yes, the

Chinese contained the virus, but at what price?" While only a whistleblower can tell us the whole story of what really went on there, the fact is that when the virus broke out in Wuhan, the authorities imposed a lockdown and halted the majority of production across the country, clearly prioritizing human lives over the economy. This happened with some delay, true, but they took the crisis extremely seriously. Now they are reaping the rewards, including economically. And let's be clear, this was only possible because the Communist Party is still able to control and regulate the economy—there is social control over market mechanisms, albeit a "totalitarian" control. The pandemic is not just a viral process, it is a process that takes place within certain economic, social, and ideological coordinates that are open to change.

According to the theory of complex systems, such systems have two opposite features: robust stable character and extreme vulnerability. These systems can accommodate great disturbances, integrating themselves and finding new balance and stability, up to a certain threshold (a "tipping point"), above which a small disturbance can cause a total catastrophe and lead to the establishment of a totally different order. For many centuries, humanity did not have to worry about its impact on the environment— nature was able to adapt itself to deforestation, to the use of coal and oil, etc. However, it seems that today we are approaching a tipping point—one cannot really be sure, since such points can only be clearly perceived once it is already too late. So we encounter a dilemma regarding the urgency to do something about today's threat of different ecological catastrophes. Either we take the threat seriously and decide to do something which, if the catastrophe does not occur, will appear ridiculous, or we do nothing, and lose everything in the case of the catastrophe. The worst choice would be taking limited measures—in this case, we will fail no matter what occurs. That is to say, the problem is that there is no middle ground in regard to the ecological catastrophe: either it will occur or it will not occur. In such a situation, talk about anticipation, precaution, and risk control tends to become meaningless since we are dealing with "unknown unknowns." We not only do not know where the tipping point is, we don't even know exactly what we do not know.

The most unsettling aspect of the ecological crisis concerns is the so-called "knowledge in the real," which can run amok. When winter is too warm, plants and animals misread the hot weather as a signal that spring has already begun and start to behave accordingly, thus not only rendering themselves vulnerable to late onslaughts of cold, but also disturbing the entire rhythm of natural reproduction. This is how one should imagine a possible catastrophe: a small-level interruption with devastating global consequences.

So, to conclude, we should respectfully follow the old Latin motto *Mortuis nihil nisi bonum* ("Of the dead, [say] nothing but good"), and we should ignore for a brief moment all the catastrophic decisions of Rumsfeld and remember him as an amateur philosopher who introduced some distinctions useful to analyze our predicament.

IS COMMUNISM
AUTHORITARIAN CAPITALISM?

On July 1, 1921, the founding congress of the Chinese Communist Party was held in Shanghai. Twelve men gathered in a villa in the French Concession, then (and now) the richest part of the city. Today, the Party has over 90 million members, and it has changed not only the history of China but the history of the entire world. The main stages in its development are well known: In late 1920, Mao Zedong took over and reoriented the Party from city workers to poor farmers; in the mid-1930s, the Long March, although a retreat, established a link between the Party and people across China; in 1949, the revolution won; from 1958 until 1975, the Great Leap Forward and the Cultural Revolution tried to enforce fast economic and social change but failed and caused millions of deaths; starting in 1978, after Mao's death, Deng Xiaoping opened the country to capitalism under continued political control by the Party. When, in the late 1980s, this economic liberalization gave birth to political demands for democratization, the Tiananmen crackdown reasserted the Party's control.

China in recent decades is arguably one of the greatest economic success stories in human history—hundreds of millions were raised from poverty into middle-class existence. How did China achieve it? The twentieth-century Left was defined by its opposition to two fundamental tendencies of modernity: the reign of capital, with its aggressive individualism and alienating dynamics; and authoritarian-bureaucratic state power. What we get in today's China is exactly the combination of these two features in an extreme form: a strong authoritarian state with wild capitalist dynamics. Ironically, China should have the most efficient form of Socialism today. Chinese authorities continue to reprint the Marxist classics, from Marx to Mao, in hundreds of thousands of copies, but if you take these texts seriously and act upon them, as some young students did when they tried to organize workers against abuses of state power, you are arrested. In today's China, one of the main functions of the Communist party is to prevent workers from organizing a resistance against capital—a wonderfully schizophrenic situation.

The irony is that for Marx, Communism arises when capitalist relations of production become an obstacle to the further development of the means of production, meaning Communism can only be secured by a (sudden or gradual) progression away from a capitalist market economy and toward a socialized economy. Deng Xiaoping's "reforms" turn Marx around, arguing that at a certain point one has to return to capitalism to enable the economic development of Socialism.

Years ago, a Chinese social theorist with links to Deng's daughter told me an interesting anecdote. When Deng was dying, an acolyte visited him and asked what he thought was his greatest act. The assistant expected the usual answer, that he would mention the economic opening he created that brought development to China. To their surprise, he answered: "No, it was that when the leadership decided to open up the economy, I resisted the temptation to go all the way and also open up political life to multiparty democracy." According to some sources, this tendency to go all the way was strong in some Party circles, and the decision to maintain Party control was in no way preordained. We should resist the liberal temptation to dream about how if China also opened up to a political democracy, its economic progress would have been even faster. What if a political democracy generated new instabilities and tensions that would have hampered economic progress? What if this (capitalist) progress was feasible only in a society dominated by a strong authoritarian power? Recall the classical Marxist thesis on early modern England: It was in the bourgeoisie's interest to leave political power to the aristocracy and to keep economic power for itself. Maybe something homologous is going on in today's China. It was in the interest of the new capitalists to leave political power to the Communist Party, the best protector of the interests of capitalism.

It may appear that between the Cultural Revolution and Deng's reforms, China went from one extreme to another. However, there is profound structural homology between the permanent self-revolutionizing Maoist and the struggle against the ossification of state structures, and the inherent dynamics of capitalism. Here, one is tempted to paraphrase Bertolt Brecht's pun: "What is the robbing of a bank compared to the founding of a new bank?" What are the violent and destructive outbursts of a Red Guard in the Cultural Revolution compared to the true Cultural Revolution, which is the permanent dissolution of all life-forms, necessitated by the capitalist reproduction? Today, the tragedy of the Great Leap Forward is that it is repeating itself as the comedy of the rapid and capitalist Great Leap Forward into modernization. The old slogan "iron foundry into every village" has re-emerged as "a skyscraper onto every street." Or, to put it in a brutally ironic way, the liquidation of the enemies in the Maoist purges gives way to the liquida-tion of the market sales ("Everything must go!").

Some naïve Leftists claim that it is the legacy of the Cultural Revolution and Maoism in general that acts as a counterforce to unbridled capitalism, prevent-ing its worst excesses and maintaining a minimum of social solidarity. What if, however, the case is exactly the opposite? What if the Cultural Revolution, with its brutal erasure of past traditions, was the "shock" that created the conditions for a capitalist explosion? What if Naomi Klein has to add China to her list of states in which a natural, military, or social catastrophe cleared the slate for a new capitalist explosion?

The supreme irony of history is thus that it was Mao himself, by tearing apart the fabric of traditional society, who created the ideological conditions for rapid capitalist development. What was his call to the people, especially the young ones, in the Cultural Revolution? "Don't wait for someone else to tell you what to do, you have the right to rebel! So think and act for yourselves, destroy cultural relics, denounce and attack not only your elders but also government and Party officials! Swipe away the repressive state mechanisms and organ-ize yourself in communes!" And Mao's call was heard—what followed was an explosion of unrestrained passion to delegitimize all forms of authority, so that, at the end, Mao had to call in the army to restore order. The paradox is thus that the key battle of the Cultural Revolution was not between the Communist Party apparatus and the denounced traditionalist enemies but between the army and the Communist Party, and the forces that Mao himself called into being.

Duane Rousselle, a Canadian sociological philosopher, perspicuously noted the basic ambiguity in the desperate search for the alternatives to capitalism: "If the radical philosophers, including Marx and Bakunin, were quick to ask, 'What about the alternatives?' then it was because they sometimes failed to see that capitalism has assumed the position of the 'alternative.' Capitalism is the alternative (to authoritarianism, dogmatism, socialism, and so on)."[80] It is not only that capitalism can only thrive through permanent self-revolutionizing, as Marx pointed out; it is that capitalism again and again emerges as the only alternative, the only way to move forward, the dynamic force that continues when social life gets stuck in a fixed form. Today, capitalism is more revolutionary than the traditional Left, which is obsessed with protecting the old achievements of the

80   Duane Rouelle, personal communication to author.

welfare state—just recall how much capitalism changed the entire texture of our societies in the last decades.

Lenin's New Economic Policy (NEP) from the early 1920s, which allowed, to a certain degree, private property and a market economy, was obviously the original model for Deng's reforms that cleared the way for a capitalist free market (under the control of the ruling Communist Party). Now, instead of a half-decade of market liberalization in China, there is already half a century of what they euphemistically call "Socialism with Chinese characteristics." So has China, for over half a century, followed a gigantic New Economic Policy? Instead of making fun of these measures or simply denouncing them as a defeat of Socialism, as a step toward (authoritarian) capitalism, we should take the risk and extend this logic to its extreme. After the disintegration of Eastern European Socialism in 1990, there was a joke that insinuated that Socialism was a transition from capitalism back to capitalism.

But what if we make the opposite move and define capitalism as a Socialist New Economic Policy, as a passage from feudalism (or premodern societies of domination in general) to Socialism? With the abolition of premodern relations of servitude and domination, with the assertion of principles such as personal freedom and human rights, capitalist modernity is in itself already Socialist. No wonder modernity, again and again, gave birth to revolts against domination, which had already pointed toward economic equality (large peasants' revolts in Germany in the early 1500s, Jacobins, etc.). Capitalism is the passage from pre-modernity to Socialism in the sense that it is the form of a compromise: It accepts the end of direct relations of domination (i.e., the principle of personal freedom and equality), but (as Marx put it in his classic formulation) it transposes domination from the relations between people to the relations between things (commodities). In other words, as individuals, we are all free, but domination persists in the relationship between commodities that we exchange on the market.

The big question that haunts us from the twentieth century is: Can you abolish market freedom without abolishing political freedom? You certainly can abolish political freedom without abolishing market freedom; China proved that. In another case of *List der Vernunft*, the Chinese Party won, but the final result of its rule seems to be to provide a new form of authoritarian capitalism that will replace liberal capitalism. Is China, then, the biggest threat to a genuine democratic emancipation?

Commentators who are eager to avoid Eurocentrism warn us that China is not a nation-state in the European sense, but a heterogeneous territory united by a shared civilization that encompasses a specific spiritual tradition as well as a thick cobweb of manners and everyday rituals. (Just think about drinking tea in contrast to drinking coffee, which is central in Western socializing.) But is this still the case? Have we not been witnessing a whole series of clear steps toward a strong nation-state? In China, there has been nationalist patriotism and distrust toward foreign (Western) cultures, resulting in things such as the imposition of Han as the official language.

This move toward the nation-state should worry us because a sovereign nation-state implies a certain stance toward war, made clear by Hegel. Each state disciplined/educated its own members and guaranteed civic peace among them in the guise of state power, but the relationship between different states was permanently under the shadow of potential war, and each period of peace was nothing more than a temporary armistice. As Hegel conceptualized it, the entire ethic of a state culminates in the highest act of heroism, the readiness to sacrifice one's life for one's nation-state, which means that the wild barbarian relations between states serve as the foundation of the ethical life within a state. Is today's North Korea, with its ruthless pursuit of nuclear weapons and rockets, not the ultimate example of unconditional nation-state sovereignty?

There are clear signs China is moving in this direction. I was informed by friends in China that authors in Chinese military journals complain that the Chinese Army needs a real war to test its fighting ability. The U.S. Army is permanently testing its ability in Iraq. For decades after the failed intervention in Vietnam, China didn't have the chance to do this. Recently, the Chinese official media openly claimed that since the prospect of a peaceful integration of Taiwan into China is dwindling, a military liberation of the island will be necessary. As they ideologically prepare for this, Chinese nationalist patriotism and suspicion of all things foreign has grown. This suspicion is accompanied by accusations that the U.S. wants war for Taiwan. In the fall of 2021, top Chinese authorities advised people to stock enough food supplies to survive for two months if, due to a non-specified event, food distribution was disturbed—a strange warning, which was generally perceived as an announcement that war was to come. Plus, one should mention the Chinese mega-hit movie *Battle at the Lake of Changjin*, which celebrates the Chinese intervention outside China's territory (in the Korean War) in 1950. Maybe even today's global capitalism needs nation-states. China is now paying the price for embracing a capitalist economy—one needs a strong nation-state to control the economy and keep society together.

What further complicates things is that tensions are also rising between Russia and Ukraine. Russia is signaling that it plans to invade Ukraine, and the two attacks (on Taiwan and Ukraine) seem coordinated. Russia is hoping that the West will not be able to sustain a double war. However, we are not taking a simple anti-Chinese and anti-Russian stance—Biden is prolonging Trump's trade war against China in the hopes of maintaining America's near-monopoly over new digital media, and the West also broke the agreement that former Soviet Union sovereign states could not join NATO. Both sides are playing an extremely dangerous game. In today's conditions, what winning a war means is best described by the title of a CNN report on Syria: "President Assad won the war but lost his country."[81] Alain Badiou wrote that the contours of the future war are already drawn:

81   CNN reporters, "Death of a Revolution," *Tug of War* (podcast), December 1, 2021, https://edition.cnn.com/audio/podcasts/tug-of-war/episodes/92a49391-aaa9-442e-9dda-adef00f75877.

The United States and their Western-Japanese clique on the one side, China and Russia on the other side, atomic arms everywhere. We cannot but recall Lenin's statement: "Either revolution will prevent the war or the war will trigger revolution." This is how we can define the maximal ambition of the political work to come: For the first time in History, the first hypothesis—revolution will prevent the war—should realize itself, and not the second one—a war will trigger revolution. It is effectively the second hypothesis which materialized itself in Russia in the context of the First World War, and in China in the context of the second. But at what price! And with what long-term consequences![82]

But how can we even imagine a revolution that will prevent the war to come? Let's stay with Badiou and his motto *mieux vaut un désastre qu'un désêtre* (better a disaster—the catastrophic outcome of an event—than a non-eventful survival in a hedonist-utilitarian universe). The origin of this motto is Julien Gracq's *The Opposing Shore* (original title: *Le Rivage des Syrtes*), a novel about Orsenna, a fictional stand-in for Italy, a country ruled

---

82 Alan Badiou, personal communication with author. My only distance from Badiou is that I would also call the Chinese-Russian axis a clique.

by the ancient and decadent city of the same name, which for the last three hundred years has been in a state of suspended war with Farghestan, the barbarian desert country across the sea to the south. The leadership of Orsenna decides to provoke an open war with Farghestan in order to break the spell of the decadent apathy and bring authentic life back to Orsenna, even though they are aware that the war will result in Orsenna's destruction. The underlying existential dilemma is: What is more desirable, an inert life of small satisfactions (not a true life at all) or taking a risk which may end in a catastrophe?

But is Gracq's example not misleading? Orsenna's hedonist non-being society is a false state that obfuscates underlying social antagonisms, and the pseudo-event of the war with Farghestan exacerbates this obfuscation. So there are three terms and not two: the event (which may end up in disaster), the pseudo-event (Fascism, or in this case, war), and the hedonist-utilitarian bio-politics of non-being, of regulating animal-human life. The difficulty today is how to distinguish the first from the second since they often share many features. Even if we agree with the formula "*mieux vaut un désastre qu'un désêtre,*" what about "*mieux vaut un pseudo-evenement qu'un désêtre*"? Is a Fascist "event" also better than a non-eventful capitalist survival? Here Badiou is walking on a dangerous edge, sometimes confusing the two. Back in the early 1990s, in a Gracq-like mode, Badiou wrote that a victory of Milošević in the post–Yugoslav War would be more interesting politically than the victory of the forces opposed to him, which was a clear preference for a nationalist pseudo-event over a non-eventful life.

It is crucial for us to discern between fundamentalist pseudo-events (mobilization for a national cause) and authentic events (struggle for social justice, against global warming, etc.). To do this is pretty easy: A pseudo-event is by definition exclusionary, a passionate defense of one's own state or ethnic or religious identity, while an authentic event is by definition universal. When there was a brief war between Azerbaijan and Armenia, I remember a report from the Armenian side in which one of their soldiers said, "We have the pandemic, but now we fight for our country, so we should forget the pandemic and focus on the war!" This comment made me very sad.

GORBACHEV'S
SECOND DEATH

Mikhail Gorbachev's biological death is his second death. Symbolically, he died with the dissolution of the Soviet Union. His role was purely a negative one, that of a vanishing mediator. He "tore down the Wall," he set in motion the disappearance of the Communist system, and he is remembered and praised for allowing this disappearance to take place in a peaceful way. Gorbachev played his role honestly, so what went wrong? Why did perestroika turn into katastroika?

When Nikita Khrushchev began his de-Stalinization in 1956, his wager was that his (limited) confession would strengthen the Communist movement, and in the short term he was right. One should always remember that the Khrushchev era was the last period of authentic Communist enthusiasm, of belief in the Communist project. During his visit to the U.S. in 1959, Khrushchev made his famous defiant statement to the American public that "your grandchildren will be Communists." In doing so, he effectively spelled out the conviction of the entire Soviet nomenklatura. His de-Stalinization was marked by a long process of "rehabilitation," of admitting the "errors" of the Party's past politics. The gradual rehabilitation of the demonized ex-leaders of the Bolsheviks can thus serve as perhaps the most sensitive index of how far (and in what direction) the "de-Stalinization" of the Soviet Union was going. The first to be rehabilitated were the high military leaders shot in 1937 (Tukhachevsky and others). The last to be rehabilitated (already in the Gorbachev era, just before the collapse of the Communist regime) was Bukharin. This last rehabilitation was a clear turn toward capitalism. He was the one who, in the '20s, advocated the pact between workers and peasants (owners of their land), launching the famous slogan "Get rich!" and opposed forced collectivization. Significantly, however, one figure was *never* rehabilitated (excluded by the Communists as well as by the anti-Communist Russian nationalists): Trotsky, the "wandering Jew" of the Revolution, the true anti-Stalin, the archenemy, opposing the idea of "building Socialism in one country" with his vision of a permanent revolution.

After Khrushchev's fall in 1964, a resigned cynicism prevailed in the Soviet Union until Gorbachev's attempt at a more radical confrontation with the past. For Gorbachev, however, Lenin remained the absolute authority until the end of the USSR, while Trotsky continued to be a non-person for a good reason. In his very last text, Christopher Hitchens wrote that "at the very end of his life, cut off in Mexico and aware of his own declining health, he [Trotsky] admitted, after the outbreak of the Second World War, that the conflict might just end without a Socialist revolution. In that event the whole Marxist-Leninist project would have to be abandoned."[83] Here is a passage from Trotsky's last text:

> We would be compelled to acknowledge that [Stalinism] was rooted not in the backwardness of the country and not in the imperialist environment, but in the congenital incapacity of the proletariat to become a ruling class. Then it would be necessary to establish in retrospect that . . . the present USSR was the precursor of a new and universal system of exploitation.

Trotsky is clear here: One must leave behind the very basic idea of the "proletarian power," of the wretched of the earth to be able to organize alternate power. "In retrospect" means that this idea was doomed from the very beginning. This is the step Gorbachev was not ready to make when he launched the slogans of glasnost

83   Christopher Hitchens, "The Old Man," *The Atlantic,* July/August 2004, https://www.theatlantic.com/magazine/archive/2004/07/the-old-man/302984/.

and perestroika—he failed to see that he unleashed an avalanche that changed the world.

With Deng Xiaoping's reforms, the Chinese proceeded in a radically different, almost opposite, way. While in the sphere of economy (and, up to a point, culture) what is usually understood as Communism was abandoned and the gates were opened wide to Western-style liberalization (private property, profit-making, hedonist individualism, etc.), the Party nevertheless maintained its ideological-political hegemony—not in the sense of doctrinal orthodoxy (in the official discourse, the Confucian reference to the "Harmonious Society" practically replaced any reference to Communism) but in the sense of maintaining the unconditional political hegemony of the Communist Party as the only guarantee for stability and prosperity in China. This required close monitoring and regulation of the ideological discourse on Chinese history, especially the history of the last two centuries. The recounting of China's recent history is varied. It includes China's humiliation in the Opium Wars, which ended only with the Communist victory in 1949, and led to the conclusion that to be patriotic is to support the rule of the Party.

When history is given such a legitimizing role, it cannot tolerate any substantial self-critique. The Chinese had learned the lesson of Gorbachev's failure: Full recognition of the "founding crimes" will only bring the entire system down. Thus, those crimes must remain disavowed. True, some Maoist "excesses" and "errors" have been denounced (such as the Great Leap Forward and the devastating famine that followed, and the Cultural Revolution), and Deng Xiaoping's assessment of Mao's role (70 percent positive, 30 percent negative) is enshrined as the official formula. But this assessment functions as a formal conclusion which renders any further elaboration superfluous. Even if Mao was 30 percent bad, the full symbolic impact of this admission would be neutralized. He would continue to be celebrated as the founding father of the nation—his body in a mausoleum and his image on every banknote. We are dealing here with a clear case of fetishistic disavowal. Although we know very well that Mao made errors and caused immense suffering, his figure is kept magically untainted by these facts. In this way, the Chinese Communists can have their cake and eat it too: The radical changes brought about by economic liberalization are combined with the continuation of the same Party rule as before.

My saddest memory about Gorbachev is a rumor that circulated in Germany in the 1990s. Who knows if it is true, but *se non e vero, e ben trovato* ("even if it is not true, it makes the right point"). On a visit to Berlin after he lost power, Gorbachev tried to make a surprise visit to the ex-chancellor Willy Brandt. However, when he (with his guards) approached Brandt's house and rang the bell, Brandt refused to see him. Later, Brandt explained to a friend why: He never forgave Gorbachev for allowing the dissolution of the Communist bloc, and not because Brandt was a secret believer in Soviet Communism, but because he was well aware that the disappearance of the Communist bloc would also mean the disappearance of the Western European Social Democratic Welfare State. That is to say, Brandt knew that the capitalist system was ready to make considerable concessions to the workers and the poor only if there was a serious threat of an alternative, of a different mode of production that promises workers their rights. To retain its legitimacy, capitalism has to demonstrate how it works better even for the workers and the poor, and the moment this alternative vanishes, one can proceed to dismantle the welfare state.

The ongoing global crisis clearly calls for radical social change. However, if we want to resuscitate the vision of a truly different Communism, it will have to be done on a totally different basis than the one imagined by Gorbachev (and Lenin).

PENG SHUAI AND THE REIGN OF PURE APPEARANCE

The story is well known, widely commented on, and widely reported in all media. On November 2, 2021, Peng Shuai, a top Chinese tennis player, posted a lengthy message on her Weibo account accusing Zhang Gaoli, a former senior Chinese vice premier and high-ranking member of the Chinese Communist Party (CCP), of sexual assault. This was the first time a member of the top echelons of the CCP faced this level of sexual misconduct allegations in public. The accusation drew attention to the #MeToo movement in China, but her post was removed within twenty minutes of being uploaded, and all discussion on Chinese social media and news outlets about the matter became subject to blanket censorship. Shuai also disappeared from public life. In reaction to growing worldwide concerns over her whereabouts and safety, official media offered some unconvincing denials and explanations that only deepened the mystery. Now the story had another turn: Gaoli was part of a group opposed to President Xi, and it seemed as if the whole incident was staged by the president and his supporters to get rid of his opponents. We were all duped by the fake sexual scandal: Shuai's post was removed after only twenty minutes—just enough time for the news to spread around the world.

This sad anecdote (and where all my sympathies go to Shuai) is not just about oppression of women in an authoritarian society. It also showcases a weird feature of Communist regimes: the obsession with appearances, which have to be maintained whatever the cost. When Deng Xiaoping was still alive, although already retired from the post of the general secretary of the CCP, one of the top nomenklatura members was purged. The official reason given to the press was that this member had divulged a state secret; namely, that Deng was still the supreme authority who made decisions. The irony of it is that this fact was common knowledge: Everybody knew that Deng was still pulling the strings; it was in all the media all the time.

This logic of appearance (which is untouchable even though everyone knows it's just an appearance) recently reached an extreme in North Korea. From time to time, we read about the North Korean media's weird claims: when Kim Il Sung died, birds descended from the sky and cried at his coffin; their leader doesn't defecate, etc. Our reactions to such claims are either that we presume ordinary people secretly laugh at this, well aware that it is nonsense, or maybe they are so brainwashed that they really believe it. But this third reaction is more convincing: What if such stories are propagated by the regime not as literal truths, but as something like folkloric tales told with respect but with the knowledge that they are fiction? There is, however, a price to be paid for respecting such appearances. A couple years ago, a young woman who was selling things at a (tolerated, although not legally permitted) flea market put the money she earned into a plastic bag and buried it in her garden. The police discovered it, she was prosecuted and condemned . . . for what? Not for black market activity or illegal financial dealings but for a wholly different reason: The plastic bag didn't fully protect the cash and it was ruined, and because the banknotes have images of their Leader, the woman was condemned for disrespectfully treating his image.

A regime of appearances was first fully established in Stalinism—we all know how absolutely crucial appearances were in Stalinism. The Stalinist regime reacted with total panic whenever there was a threat that appearances would be disturbed (like if an accident showing the failure of the regime could be reported in the public media). In the Soviet media there were no black chronicles, no reports on crimes and prostitution, not to mention workers or public protests. Let's just recall why it never rained during the First of May parades in Moscow. The authorities feared that if rain disturbed the parade, it would be perceived as an indication that the Party was not all-powerful, so the authorities sprayed the sky above Moscow with gasses that prevented the formation of clouds. What characterizes Stalinism is precisely this combination of raw brutal terror and the need to protect appearances—even if we all know something is not true, the big Other (of appearances) should not notice it.

In this order of appearances, prohibitions themselves are prohibited. In Stalin's time, it was prohibited not only to criticize Stalin but also to publicly announce this prohibition. Is it not similar in the case of Peng Shuai? What we get from official sources is not even a clear denial— something like: "Zhang Gaoli never sexually molested Peng Shuai"—instead, we get erasure, and at best, denial of something that is not clearly stated, only referred to as "that rumor," or "what people are talking about."

In today's populist West, we seem to find ourselves at the opposite extreme. Traditionally (or in our retroactive view of tradition, at least), shameless obscenity worked subversively, undermining traditional domination and depriving the Master of their false dignity. I remember from my own youth how protesting students liked to use obscene words or gestures to embarrass figures of power and, so they claimed, denounce their hypocrisy. However, today's explosion of public obscenity is not causing the authority or Master figures to disappear; rather, it is resulting in their forceful reappearance. We are getting something that was unimaginable decades ago: obscene Masters. But this obscenity is counterbalanced by the politically correct discourse in which, as in Stalinism, "prohibitions themselves are prohibited"—when something is erased, one does not want to admit that it was done for ideological reasons, so a more neutral reason is given. On September 5, 2021, the *Guardian* published a long interview with Judith Butler. Less than two days later, a part of the interview—in which Butler called trans-exclusionary radical feminists (TERFs) "fascists"—disappeared and in its place there was a note: "This article was edited on September 7, 2021 to reflect developments which occurred after the interview took place."[84] No specifications of how some new

84 Walker Caplan, "*The Guardian* published a Judith Butler interview—and then deleted an answer about TERFS." *Literary Hub*, September 9, 2021, https://lithub.com/the-guardian-published-a-judith-butler-interview-and-then-deleted-a-part-that-condemned-gender-critical-transphobia/.

incident could problematize Butler's principled answer were given. Clearly the article was censored due to TERF pressure, but this reason had to be concealed because it would give rise to allegations of ideological censorship.

The choice between fidelity to appearances and public obscenity is a difficult one, and the stakes are very high. But it is ultimately a false choice: Both sides are wrong. They both came out of the disintegration of the social big Other, the set of customs and values that determines the basic features of decency in our social contracts. When the big Other disintegrates, the choice is between obscenity and enforced group terror.

In the famous passage of Immanuel Kant's "What Is Enlightenment?" he opposes the "public" and the "private" use of reason. Private is not one's individual space as opposed to communal ties, but the very communal-institutional order of one's particular identification, while public is the trans-national universality of the exercise of one's reason. This is why Kant's formula of Enlightenment is neither "Don't obey, think freely!" nor "Don't obey, think and rebel!" but "Think freely, state your thoughts publicly, *and obey!*" The same holds for vaccine skeptics: Debate, publish your doubts, but obey regulations once the public authority imposes them. Without practical consensus we will slowly drift into a society composed of tribal factions, as is happening in many Western countries. But without the space for the public use of reason, the state itself courts the danger of becoming just another instance of the private use of reason.

At the beginning of the Covid outburst we saw the price a society had to pay for the absence of the public space of reason. Because the scientists who first discovered the virus were silenced, China lost precious months in which it could have limited the pandemic to a local incident. And now, apropos Shuai, we should raise a similar question: How come a political struggle (which should have been fought out in open) has to take the appearance of a sexual scandal?

The challenge for us today—while a multiparty democracy is clearly less and less able to confront our big challenges like climate change—is: How to maintain the space for the public use of reason outside multiparty democracy in the Western liberal sense?

IS SOLIDARITY ANTI-SEMITIC?

The Europe worth defending is the Europe of universal solidarity, not just the Europe of selective solidarity with those who "like us." On January 3, 2022, Emma Watson, a star best known as Hermione in the *Harry Potter* films, posted on Instagram an image of a pro-Palestinian rally overlaid with the words "Solidarity is a verb" and a quotation from Sara Ahmed on the meaning of solidarity (which does not mention Jews or Palestinians): "Solidarity does not assume that our struggles are the same struggles, or that our pain is the same pain, or that our hope is for the same future. Solidarity involves commitment, and work, as well as the recognition that even if we do not have the same feelings, or the same lives, or the same bodies, we do live on common ground." Immediately, Watson's Instagram post sparked accusations of anti-Semitism from Israeli politicians. It got so bad that even the big Western media like CNN had to admit that the accusations had gone too far.[85]

85   Jack Guy, "Emma Watson's pro-Palestinian Instagram post sparks 'anti-Semitism' spat," *CNN,* January 5, 2022, https://edition.cnn.com/2022/01/05/entertainment/emma-watson-antisemitism-instagram-scli-intl/index.html.

This incident makes it obvious that the official Israeli stance, according to which a critique of the Israeli policy is okay but not when it becomes anti-Semitic, is a lie. The reality is that no matter how innocent and neutral a critique of Israel may sound, the defenders of Israel and its politics always find some metaphoric or metonymic link to anti-Semitism. This stance reaches an extreme in the claim that a critique of capitalism is anti-Semitic, because in our popular imagination Jews are identified with financial wealth. So the truth of the distinction between a critique of Israeli policy and anti-Semitism is that there is none: Every critique de facto echoes anti-Semitism; an acceptable critique of Israel is an empty set (in the mathematical sense of the set theory). In the case of Watson, this logic is brought to the extreme. We don't have to look for anything behind or beneath—the mere mention of solidarity, when applied to what the state of Israel is doing with Palestinians, becomes anti-Semitic. However, the same accusation could and should also be made against the reactions to Watson's post. When they accuse Watson of being anti-Semitic for promoting solidarity, are they silently assuming that solidarity itself is anti-Semitic? But if solidarity is in itself anti-Semitic, then it becomes something that must be foreign to Judaism.

The problem here is the asymmetry implied by the partisans of Israeli politics, who practice the wildest hermeneutics of suspicion, discovering traces of anti-Semitism everywhere. And yet, sympathizers of West Bank Palestinians are not allowed to criticize them, to bring out the apartheid and oppression at work in "neutral" Israeli security measures, without being called anti-Semitic. Yes, one should be horrified at Iran's project to destroy Israel, but one should be no less horrified by what Israel is doing to West Bank Palestinians.

The title of a recent dialogue on anti-Semitism and BDS on *Der Spiegel* was: "Wer Antisemit ist, bestimmt der Jude und nicht der potenzielle Antisemit" ("Who is an anti-Semite is determined by the Jew and not the potential anti-Semite").[86] Okay, sounds logical, the victim should decide if they are really a victim. But there are two problems here: (1) Should not the same also hold for Palestinians who should be able to determine who is stealing their land and depriving them of elementary

86   Michael Wolffsohn and Michael Naumann, »Wer Antisemit ist, bestimmt der Jude und nicht der potenzielle Antisemit,« interview by Christoph Schult and Severin Weiland, *Spiegel Politics*, December 18, 2020, https://www.spiegel.de/politik/ deutschland/michael-wolffsohn-und-michael-naumann-im-streitgespraech-wer-antisemit-ist-bestimmt-der-jude-a-00000000-0002-0001-0000-000174544040.

rights? (2) Who is "the Jew" who determines who is an anti-Semite? What about the numerous Jews who support BDS, or who have doubts about Israel's politics regarding the West Bank? Does the quoted claim from *Der Spiegel* not imply that the Jews who are critical of the politics of Israel towards the Palestinians are betraying their Jewish identity? No wonder they are often called "self-hating Jews" . . .

WELCOME TO THE AGE OF ARTIFICIAL SCARCITY!

The best indication of the change that affects our financial system is the rise of two new interrelated phenomena: Bitcoin and NFTs (*NFT* was the Collins word of the year in 2021). Bitcoin and NFTs both emerged out of a libertarian idea to bypass state apparatuses and establish direct communication between concerned parties. In both cases we see how the idea turned into its opposite: Bitcoin and NFTs have their own 1 percent who dominate and manipulate the field. Here we should avoid both praising Bitcoin and NFTs as a new space of freedom and dismissing them as the latest speculative capitalist madness.

First, Bitcoin. Our usual experience with money is that its value is guaranteed by some state authority like the central bank, and that the state can also misuse this authority (printing money and causing inflation, etc.). In the case of Bitcoin, its value is not guaranteed by any public institution of authority, but determined by what people will pay for it—and they are ready to pay for it if they believe in it, if they trust it. Here, in the domain of cold and ruthless financial speculations, belief and trust enter the stage. Bitcoins are like an ideological cause which exists as a real force only if enough people believe in it—without individuals who believe in the Communist cause there is no Communism, for example. There's a similarity to how stocks are priced, but the difference is that in principle the value of stocks is not purely self-referential; it refers to investments which are expected to generate profit from "real" production. If one wants the price of a stock to fall, one spreads false news about a company that issues that stock. There is no such reference with Bitcoins. This doesn't mean that the amount of Bitcoins is limitless: The protocol established by Bitcoin founder Satoshi Nakamoto dictates that only 21 million Bitcoins can ever be mined (almost 19 million have been mined so far). There is a limited supply, like with gold and other precious metals, but no intrinsic "real value." How can this be? Bitcoins have to be registered in blockchains, which are:

> essentially decentralized ledgers. They're a "place" to store information, and crucially, because they are decentralized, cannot be edited without the knowledge of other users on the blockchain. The idea is that blockchains are able to store records of information without the need for third parties

(e.g., banks and financial institutions), so that the system is essentially self-sufficient and self-regulating. As a digital infrastructure, an added benefit is that huge legal fees added by third parties are avoided.[87]

Here we stumble upon the tension that defines blockchains: Precisely because there is no third party, because the system is essentially self-sufficient and self-regulating, every registration/inscription of a new Bitcoin involves a tremendous amount of work through which the new Bitcoin will be brought to "the knowledge of other users on the blockchain." Since there is no third party to which every Bitcoin owner could refer, each new owner has to develop a complex texture of algorithms and codes which guarantee that the specific identity of the new Bitcoin will be clearly perceived by all others without making it turn into something that can be appropriated by others. A blockchain as a non-alienated big "Other" needs a lot more than inscription into an alienated third party, making the Bitcoin "miners" who do this work the "proletarians" in the new domain.

---

87 "The NFT: A Wealth and Poverty of Imagination," Aesthetics for Birds, March 18, 2021, https://aestheticsforbirds.com/2021/03/18/nfts-a-wealth-and-poverty-of-imagination/.

We've gone from old miners (who do their difficult work deep beneath the earth) as the nineteenth-century typical figure of a proletarian to Bitcoin miners, who work to construct and secure the space for a Bitcoin in the digital big Other. The paradox here is that they do not work to produce new use values, but to create new space for exchange value—to guarantee that Bitcoins do not need a legal external authority and the accompanying legal fees. This work takes a lot of time and uses so much energy (electricity) that an individual who mines for Bitcoin creates a greater ecological burden and pollutes our environment more than a miner digging for coal.[88]

The potentially progressive idea of Bitcoin as global and independent of state apparatuses actualizes itself in a form that undermines its premise. It is similar with NFTs, which were also invented as a decentralized, anti-State libertarian attempt to preserve the autonomy of artists from institutional clutches. The price we pay for this idea is that "the creation of an NFT is an attempt to create artificial scarcity where there is none. Anyone can create an NFT for a digital asset, even if there's no

---

88 "The Environmental Impacts of Cryptomining," Earthjustice, September 23, 2023, https://earthjustice.org/feature/ cryptocurrency-mining-environmental-impacts.

actual asset behind it!"[89] The paradox of NFTs is that they introduce scarcity into a domain in which items are accessible to everyone for free; for this reason, NFTs compel us to rethink the notion of property, of owning something in a digital space:

> Through subscription services, we have temporary access, but never own a thing. In some quite important sense we might ask, were we to own something, what would it be? An original master of a film or music? Perhaps. But in reality what we can say is ours is either the temporary access, or a download. The download is likely to be absolutely identical to every other download that exists. In other words, our owning it doesn't preclude others from owning it. This is why even the thought of owning a piece of art online has a tinge of absurdity about it. If the song exists as a file, it can exist identically in an infinite number of digital spaces. But NFTs provide a kind of "solution": artificial scarcity. They give us digital collectibles in a world where duplication has zero costs.[90]

89   Nelson Wan, "NFTs and SPACs: the insanity of casino capitalism," *Socialist Appeal*, March 31, 2021, https://socialist.net/nfts-and-spacs-the-insanity-of-casino-capitalism/.

90   "The NFT: A Wealth and Poverty of Imagination," Aesthetics for Birds.

What is intriguing with NFTs is the idea of taking a digital asset that anyone can copy and claiming ownership of it. An NFT has almost no use value (maybe it brings some social prestige to owners); what sustains it is its potential future exchange value. It is a copy with a price, an item of purely symbolic ownership that can bring profit. The key Hegelian insight here (as well as in the case of Bitcoin) is that although Bitcoin and NFTs appear as anomalies (as a pathological deviation from the "normal" functioning of money and commodities), the two effectively actualize a potentiality that is already contained in the very notion of commodity and money.

Partisans of crypto and NFTs are ready to admit that Bitcoin and NFTs are not anomalies but a logical consequence of the economy based on commodity exchanges, but they don't see how the "libertarian" crypto necessarily gives birth to new forms of centralized control. They dismiss such new forms of domination as contingent anomalies. Peter Thiel is a perfect example, to whom "Artificial Intelligence is communist and crypto is libertarian"—why? Because with AI,

> . . . you're sort of going to have the big eye of Sauron watching you at all times, in all places . . . The main AI applications that people seem to talk about are using large data to sort of

monitor people, know more about people than they know about themselves . . . where you can know enough about people that you know more about them than they know about themselves, and you can sort of enable communism to work, maybe not so much as an economic theory, but at least as a political theory. So it is definitely a Leninist thing. And then, it is literally communist because China loves AI.[91]

Sounds evident and convincing. However, as Thom Dunn duly noted,

Thiel's big critique here does seem to be about the authoritarian use of data and surveillance. Which, okay, cool, I agree, that's a valid concern. I don't know what that has to do [with] a revolutionary vanguard party forming a transitional state in order to establish a classless and leaderless society, but, um, sure. China does technically call itself a government. So I think I get what he's putting down here. But just so we're clear: this is the guy who helped found Palantir. Like, the big data analytics company that literally ICE [hired] to organize

91   Thom Dunn, "Peter Thiel claims AI is 'Leninist' and 'literally communist' in a sprawling speech for a think tank," *BoingBoing*, December 3, 2023, https://boingboing.net/2019/12/03/peter-thiel-claims-ai-is-len.html.

its authoritarian tactics. Which is the same Peter
Thiel who also founded the Anduril surveillance
company, and used his billions to destroy a successful news organization for criticizing him. And
he's afraid of AI because of . . . communism?[92]

It is impossible to miss the irony here: The libertarian anti-Leninist Thiel relies on the very "Leninist" AI
mechanisms he deplores. This is why one of the true
heroes of our time is Christopher Wylie, a gay Canadian
vegan who, at twenty-four, came up with an idea that led
to Cambridge Analytica. He was a key figure in digital
operations during Donald Trump's election campaign
and created Steve Bannon's psychological warfare tool.[93]
Wylie's plan was to break into Facebook (now Meta) and
use the private and personal information of millions of
people in the U.S. to create sophisticated psychological
and political profiles that would target them with political ads.[94] At a certain point Wylie was genuinely freaked

92 Ibid.

93 David Smith, "How Trump won the election: volatility
    and a common touch," *The Guardian*, November 9, 2016,
    https://www.theguardian.com/us-news/2016/nov/09/
    how-did-donald-trump-win-analysis.

94 Carole Cadwalladr and Emma Graham-Harrison, "How
    Cambridge Analytica turned Facebook 'likes' into a

out: "It's insane. The company has created psychological profiles of 230 million Americans. And now they want to work with the Pentagon? It's like Nixon on steroids."[95] What makes this story so fascinating is that it combines elements that we usually perceive as opposites. The alt-Right presents itself as a movement that addresses the concerns of ordinary white, hard-working, deeply religious people who stand for simple traditional values and abhor corrupted eccentrics, like homosexuals and vegans, but also digital nerds. Now, their electoral triumphs were masterminded and orchestrated precisely by such a nerd who stands for all that they oppose.

There is no contradiction between Thiel's anti-Leninism and Bannon's Leninism if we understand "Leninism" as total digital control over a population. Both men practice this while maintaining a libertarian face. The difference resides only in the fact that for Bannon, "Leninism" means the destruction of the state

lucrative political tool," *The Guardian*, March 17, 2018, https://www.theguardian.com/technology/2018/mar/17/facebook-cambridge-analytica-kogan-data-algorithm.

95   Carole Cadwalladr, "'I made Steve Bannon's psychological warfare tool': meet the data war whistleblower," *The Guardian*, March 18, 2018, https://www.theguardian.com/news/2018/mar/17/data-war-whistleblower-christopher-wylie-faceook-nix-bannon-trump.

and its apparatuses (without, of course, really intending it). Here, we must go to the end: Digital control and manipulation are not anomalies or deviations from today's libertarian project; they are its necessary frame, its formal condition of possibility. The system can afford the appearance of freedom only under the conditions of digital and other modes of control that regulate our freedom. For the system to function, we *must* remain formally free and perceive ourselves as free, too.

AOC AND HER
BOYFRIEND'S FEET

In late December 2021, the American nationalist Rightist Steve Cortes tweeted a photo of Alexandria Ocasio-Cortez (AOC) and her boyfriend, Riley Roberts, enjoying their Christmas break in Florida. Cortes wrote: "Her guy is showing his gross pale male feet in public – not at a pool or beach – with hideous sandals." AOC quipped back: "If Republicans are mad they can't date me, they can just say that instead of projecting their sexual frustrations onto my boyfriend's feet. Ya creepy weirdos."[96] Her reply triggered mixed reactions. One user responded: "Bold move . . . when people disagree with my policy positions or call me a hypocrite, I tell them they just want to f. . . me as well." Another responded, "Why did your mind automatically go to 'dating you' and 'sex'? That's very conceited."[97]

96   Stacy M. Brown, "Ocasio-Cortez Blasts 'Sexual Frustrations' of Republicans Criticizing Miami Beach Photo," *Washington Informer*, December 31, 2021, https://www.washingtoninformer.com/ocasio-cortez-blasts-sexual-frustrations-of-republicans-criticizing-miami-beach-photo/.

97   Srivats Lakshman, "Did AOC REALLY say Republican men want to have sex with her? BF feet tweet creates uproar," *MEAWW*, December 31, 2021, https://meaww.com/aoc-tweet-steve-cortes-boyfriend-feet-troll-internet-reactions.

At some level these reactions were right; AOC brought sex into a situation that was not sexualized (explicitly, at least). Incidentally, I don't think the reasoning implied by AOC is correct—there is another more probable version. Her Republican critics primarily disagree with her policies, but they also notice her sexual attractiveness, so they bring in sexuality to devalue her arguments. This is in accordance with the standard male-chauvinist wisdom that beautiful women are stupid: "Stick to sex, avoid argumentation which is beyond your league . . . " The implicit reference to foot fetishism (Roberts's foot really does protrude a little bit excessively in the photo) is even more ambiguous. Cortes (who made this move from AOC to Roberts's foot) could have made AOC mad for another unexpected reason—instead of really desiring her (as AOC's reply suggests), he seems to prefer her partner to her. The implicit surmise of her reply could thus be: "I am the real beauty in the photo, so why did you mention my boyfriend's foot and not me?"

Such tensions indicate that a truly radical feminist should do what Amia Srinivasan proposes in her path-breaking book, *The Right to Sex*.[98] Srinivasan writes that "beyond the parameters of consent," she is

98 Amia Srinivasan, *The Right to Sex* (New York: Farrar, Straus and Giroux, 2021).

not afraid to confront sex in all its complexity and ambiguity. Consent? Yes, but why is it always the woman
who gives consent or denies it? Why should a woman
not be the active part in a seduction, not just reacting to
male advances? Plus, consent relies on a logic of market
exchange. "The idea of consent presupposes a contract:
Someone is asking to do something to you, and they
have to get permission to do it."[99] To that end, consen-
sual sex can also be exploitative. And what about my
unconscious, which can make me desire things I do not
know, including a desire to humiliate others and myself?
What if suffering brings a perverse pleasure? And what
about the social dimension of desire? Is my intimate
desire not always affected by public and secret social
norms and expectations? The image of a sexual partner who is perceived as "desirable" obviously depends
on the society in which I live. For example, Srinivasan
concludes: "We need a feminism that is truly interna-
tionalist, that centres on climate disaster, colonialism,
and the voices of women in the global south."[100]

99   Srinivasan, *The Right to Sex*, 14.

100 Dominique Sisley, "The Right To Sex: How Amia Srinivasan
     Wrote the Most Divisive Book of 2021," *AnOther*, August 25, 2021,
     https://www.anothermag.com/design-living/13510/the-right-to-
     sex-how-amia-srinivasan-wrote-the-most-divisive-book-of-2021.

Here is such a case from the "global south," a terrifying event that took place on the morning of January 26, 2022 in a New Delhi neighborhood in India.[101] A young woman, the mother of a three-year-old child, was attacked by a mob in her parent's house. Her hair was chopped off and her face blackened; she was brutally slapped and kicked as others in the house clapped and cheered. The attack continued for several minutes as the woman pleaded for mercy, her body crouched and hands folded. After the beating she was paraded in the narrow lanes of the neighborhood and dragged by the mob to her "victim's" house, where she was gang-raped. And who was her victim? The attack took place because the woman had repeatedly rejected the advances of a teenager who lived next to her parent's home. The sixteen-year-old boy's family claims he killed himself following her rejection in November 2021. The teen's death caused the purported "revenge attack."

There are two notably shocking moments in this affair. First, a video shared on social media shows that most of the baying mob were women. When the

101   Bilal Kuchay, "Outrage as woman allegedly gang-raped, paraded in India's capital," *Al Jazeera*, February 1, 2022, https://www.aljazeera.com/news/2022/2/1/india-new-delhi-alleged-gang-rape-torture-woman-revenge-attack.

brutalized woman was raped, it was women in the room who encouraged the men to be more brutal with her. Second, she was punished for refusing the boy's advances, even though she was married. As her sister put it, "She didn't do anything." One can only imagine what would have happened if she were to concede and give the boy a so-called mercy-fuck. If found out, she would have again been found guilty and perhaps even more brutally punished. In short, she had a choice—both options would result in catastrophe. The reactions to the incident are mostly accounted for in terms of "internalized patriarchy." In patriarchal societies women are taught they're ultimately to blame for any wrongdoing, and the scale of internalized misogyny is very large in India, where women are taught to uphold patriarchal structures.[102]

However, this explanation seems too smooth. It is ridiculous to account for the violence women exert on other women in the terms of internalized patriarchal values. What about the intense envy, hatred, and violence a woman can direct at her sexual competitors?

102 Esha Mitra, "Some people in a cheering crowd called for her to be raped. Many were women," *CNN*, February 5, 2022, https://edition.cnn.com/2022/02/04/india/india-delhi-rape-victim-shamed-intl-dst-hnk/index.html.

While this dimension is obviously not part of some eternal "woman's nature," historically it has been mediated by the patriarchal order. This dependence in no way implies that a woman's envy and violence directed at her competitors is somehow "unauthentic"—as if a woman is not able to desire and actively pursue a man and thus hate her feminine competitors. In 2019, a scandal shook Slovenia. Danijela Ružič, a judge in Maribor, the northeastern town in Slovenia, was brutally beaten in front of her house while returning home deep in the night. For some days her life was in danger. The rumor was that her partner did it because the two were ending their relationship. Angelca Likovič, an old Christian conservative politician, reacted on Facebook, writing, "She got what she deserved!" (She deserved to be beaten for her "immoral" behavior because she was allegedly returning home from a meeting with a lover).[103] Again, the shock was that it was a woman who reacted so brutally—even conservative politicians distanced themselves from her comment.

103 Razburila Javnost, "Likovičeva šokirala po napadu na sodnico: »Dobila je to, kar si je zaslužila«," *slovenske novice*, updated June 26, 2019, https://www.slovenskenovice.si/novice/slovenija/ likoviceva-sokirala-po-napadu-na-sodnico-dobila-je-to-kar-si-je-zasluzila/.

Furthermore, to make a woman responsible for a man's suicide just because she didn't gratify his (illicit) desire for sex, while simultaneously blaming her if she were to gratify it, attributes to women (at least those who are considered "attractive") an extraordinary power, which reduces men to helpless puppets. Why isn't the sixteen-year-old boy blamed for not being able to resist his desire? The true patriarchal moment of this horrible story resides also in the fact that the woman's sexual desire is never mentioned. To be direct, what if she also desired an adventure with the young boy, but was prohibited from doing it because of her fidelity to her husband? Many praise her for this fidelity, but did the same hold for her husband? Her sister emphasizes that she did nothing, but what if she were to do something in accordance with her desire about which we know nothing? To put it in vulgar terms, she was beaten and raped because she refused to cheat on her husband. Ironically, she was held responsible for NOT consenting to extramarital harassment. This perverted reversal is the hidden truth of patriarchal ethics.

Are we not now at the opposite end of the conflict around AOC's boyfriend's naked leg in Florida? Does AOC's trip to Florida not appear to be a trifling minor affair compared to what happened in New Delhi? Yes, but there is something that unites the two cases: Upon closer look, they both challenge the obvious account that offers itself. Cortes's critique of AOC as well as her reaction brings out not only the hidden male-chauvinist logic of the new Right, but also the inconsistencies of the liberal-Leftist approach to sexuality. The scandalous affair in India is not just the outcome of "primitive" patriarchal traditionalism: It could only have happened in today's mixture of traditionalism and modernity. Only within such a mixture can a woman be perceived as endowed with extraordinary powers rendering a man her helpless victim, and at the same time as deprived of her own desire.

The conclusion to be drawn is thus that while patriarchy and other forms of oppression of women (even in the guise of false "permissiveness") should be ruthlessly examined and punished, sexuality remains a big mess. It relies on rules and their codified violations, so it is impossible to fully regulate; we have to learn to live with its crazy paradoxes. We cannot ever be sure of the consequences of our interventions (as well-meant as they are). In January 2022, the Royal Opera House in London announced that it was "consulting with Ita O'Brien—an intimacy coordinator who ensures actors feel comfortable during such scenes—for Katie Mitchell's new production of *Theodora* . . . 'There's consent each and every day. You might agree one day that you're very happy to kiss lip to lip, and then you develop a cold sore, so it's not suitable anymore. So you explore what the moment is about, different ways to tell the same story,' she said."[104] While one should support the fight against any form of harassment, there are some details in this announcement that make *me* feel very uncomfortable. First, why, again, the (implicit) reduction of women to victims of harassment? Second, while obviously there are scenes in which playing a victim of rape or violence could traumatize the actor, how could one enact on screen or stage a brutal scene without feeling uncomfortable? Third, the example mentioned ("you might agree one day that you're very happy to kiss lip to lip, and then you develop a cold sore, so it's not suitable anymore") is ridiculously obvious and has nothing to do with harassment. Instead, it casts a strange light on the entire argument by putting a cold sore in the same series with, say, touching a breast of an actress. Fourth, the very term "intimacy coordinator" sounds (and is) ominous.

104 Nadia Khomami, "Royal Opera House hires intimacy coordinator for sex scenes," *The Guardian*, January 29, 2022, https://www. theguardian.com/culture/2022/jan/29/royal-opera-house-hires-intimacy-coordinator-ita-obrien-handel-theodora-sex-scenes.

At the end of this road lurks the question that even when a couple is alone and intimate, but not sure about how to interact, should they hire an intimacy coordinator?

What sustains the need for such coordinators is a desperate attempt to control and regulate sexuality. Christiane Alberti characterizes the #MeToo censorship of language as a stance directed against phallic virility, but does the phallus (in the Lacanian sense) really stand for virility?[105] The target of many #MeToo interventions is the inconsistent chaos of language games invented by sexual and power relations. In short, the #MeToo movement's control is an attempt to purify language by way of using the utmost "masculine" procedure of totalizing control and regulation. We get here a nice example of how the very critique of the masculine phallic universe proceeds in a phallic way.

So let me conclude with a lighter example, a misunderstanding that happened to a philosopher friend of mine. One of his female students said to him jokingly after a lecture, "If you explain all this to me in private, you can have sex with me!" He took a restrained stance

105   Christiane Alberti, "Lacanian Opinion (I)," *Lacanian Review Online*, March 24, 2021, https://www.thelacanianreviews.com/lacanian-opinion-i/?fbclid=IwAR0w4N4EubiNmtmVSp97pizHqd ghbQsDYJvTW8lVYAAZ4QRxsAlsFNICMCI.

and explained things to her, but with no sex, claiming that doing it to get sex as a payment would amount to sexual exploitation. Later, however, he learned from her friends that, far from being impressed by his honesty, she was furious at him—she really wanted sex, and she just playfully mentioned the price he would have to pay to avoid the vulgarity of directly asking for sex. So, again, what if women are not just victims of male predators but are also able to subtly provoke them? And why shouldn't they do this? Why should they just be passive receivers who consent or not?

CONCLUSION:

THE TROUBLE WITH PAN-ASIANISM

In an interview on a Russian state-TV channel on April 6, 2023, Viktor Bout—an international arms dealer who made headlines after he was party to a prisoner exchange between the U.S. and Russia for basketball star Brittney Griner—told a reporter he had sent a telegram to Trump urging him to flee to Russia for safety. "Most likely he will simply be eliminated there [the U.S.]. Therefore, I think it's in the best interests of all of humanity and primarily all of the American people to invite Donald Trump here, to Russia, to give him security and protection here so that he leads this uprising against the globalists and, most important, does not allow the elimination of the American people."[106] Absurd as it may sound, the proposal for a direct alliance between today's Russia and the Trumpian populism (alliance in their shared "uprising against the globalists") emulates Russia's ideological

106 Nick Reynolds, "Russia's 'Merchant of Death' Warns Donald Trump His Life Is in Danger," *Newsweek*, April 7, 2023, https://www.newsweek.com/russias-merchant-death-warns-donald-trump-his-life-danger-1793211.

project—to create a new multipolar world in which even the people in the states that dominate the global order will be liberated. Recall Trump's motto "America First!" which he also used in his short comment on why he didn't put more pressure on Saudi Arabia after the brutal murder of Jamal Khashoggi in Istanbul. Trump's argumentation is that Saudi Arabia offered special low prices to the U.S. for its petrol, so who cares about the peculiarities of the Saudi political order.[107]

That's why Trump's move to Russia is "in the best interest of all of humanity and primarily all of the American people" and the only way to prevent "the elimination of the American people"[108] by the ruling globalists. So when Putin says, "America has nothing to offer the world except domination," he is attacking America as a global power, which at the same time exploits the majority of the American people (for whom Trump speaks). America following the "America First!" policy would fit Putin's vision perfectly. During his

107 Julian E. Barnes, "Trump's Statement on Saudi Arabia, Explained!" *The New York Times*, November 20, 2018, https://www.nytimes.com/2018/11/20/us/politics/trump-statement-saudi-arabia-explained.html.

108 Reynolds, "Russia's 'Merchant of Death' Warns Donald Trump His Life Is in Danger."

annual speech to the Discussion Club on October 27, 2022, Putin criticized the U.S. and its allies in the West and called on other countries in the non-aligned world to join Russia in building a new multipolar world: "Real democracy in a multipolar world first of all presupposes the possibility for any nation, any society, and any civilization to choose their own way, their own sociopolitical system. If the United States, the European Union countries have this right, then the Asian countries, the Islamic states, the monarchies of the Persian Gulf, the states of other continents certainly have it as well."

In an abstract sense these claims may sound convincing. Democracy is not just a form of political life within a country; it can only work if each country has the right to choose its own socio-political system freely—in this sense, each country should put its interests first. When Putin and Xi Jinping met in Moscow on March 21, 2023, they made the same point. Their meeting "showed the two countries' commitment to creating a new world order, one where the U.S. is no longer the arbiter of everything that happens on the global stage."[109]

109 Robyn Dixon, "As Xi visits Russia, Putin sees his anti-U.S. world order taking shape," *The Washington Post*, March 19, 2023, https://www.washingtonpost.com/world/2023/03/19/putin-xi-russia-china-world-order/.

But what about, say, the protests in Iran? We have to accept the fact that a reference to Western democracy and human rights can *also* serve as an index of authentic protest—protesters may use this reference even if their activity is not in any way "Eurocentric."

However, China cannot be said to advocate for the Russian version of the new world order. For over a century it has been promoting another project, so-called Pan-Asianism. Pan-Asianism emerged toward the end of the nineteenth century as a reaction against Western imperialism, domination, and exploitation. From the very beginning, it was a complex project of economic and political emancipation based on the rejection of Western liberal individualism. It came in many shades, but its main ingredient was anti(-Western)-imperialism, the idea that Asia does not have to follow the Western way of progress (i.e., that it can appropriate its premodern traditions to organize its own industrial modernization in a way that will be even more dynamic than that of the West).

Viren Murthy proposes a Hegelian reading of Pan-Asianism.[110] While Hegel saw Asia as the domain

110   Viren Murthy, *Pan-Asianism and the Legacy of the Chinese Revolution* (Chicago: Chicago University Press, 2023).

of a substantial order with no space for free subjectivity, revolutionary Asian theorists propose a new Hegelian triad: The West offers abstract individualism that negates Asian substantial order and leads to social disintegration, so that only a "sublation" (*Aufhebung*, or creative overcoming) of Western individualist subjectivity in a new collective agency can give rise to new freedom. A possible solution for our catastrophic situation thus resides not in Western freedoms but in the Asian radicalization of European subjectivity. However, did we not get with Japan's militarization and colonialist expansion the first model of new radicalized collective subjectivity? Does such subjectivity not also perfectly fit Fascism?

Murthy himself points out that Pan-Asianism oscillated between its Socialist and Fascist version (the two were not often clearly divided). We should not forget that "anti-imperialism" is not as innocent a motto as it may appear: Both Japanese and German Fascists regularly used it, presenting themselves as defenders against American, British, and French imperialism. Even Sun Yat-sen, the hero of progressive Pan-Asianism, occasionally expressed sympathies for nascent European Fascism, clearly preferring it to liberalism, which he dismissed as unfit for Asian circumstances. In China, the literary and philosophical reforms of the nineteenth century gave way to the anti-Marxist developmental nationalism of Sun Yat-sen. The similarities between Italian Fascism and Sun Yat-sen's revolutionary ideology derive from their shared reactive and developmental nationalism.[111] And this tendency is discernible even in post–Deng Xiaoping China. A. James Gregor developed the thesis that today's People's Republic of China is best classified as "a variant of contemporary Fascism."[112] It is true that parts of the Latin American radical Left define their goal as a return to the ancient Incan community, but it is the same project of going "back to the future" that Putin and his clique are trying to enact in Russia (and around it) today.

For Pan-Asians who want to remain Marxists, the main point of reference is Marx's letter to Vera Zasulich, in which he allows for the possibility that collectively owned farms in Russia could directly enter Socialism without a

---

[111]   William A. Joseph, "A Place in the Sun: Marxism and Fascism in China's Long Revolution," *American Political Science Review* 95, no.1 (March 2001): 235, https://link.gale.com/apps/doc/A73021466/AONE?u=anon~73db5be&sid=googleScholar&xid=66d9ae0d.

[112]   A. James Gregor, *A Place in the Sun: Marxism and Fascism in China's Long Revolution* (New York: Routledge, 2000).

detour through capitalist de-collectivization. However, for Marx, such cases are exceptions: Only capitalism creates the proletarian, in the sense of "substance-less subjectivity," i.e., a revolutionary force able to reappropriate the alienated social substance. Premodern communities of farmers can directly pass into Socialism only when the political power of proletarians opens up the possibility for socialized agriculture. Without proletarian power, farmers cannot directly enter Socialism.

Today, the main promoter of Communist Pan-Asianism is Wang Hui, an outstanding Chinese thinker who, while faithful to Maoist legacy, is a Social Democrat in regard to the economy.[113] Wang insists that what we are witnessing today is not a result of the market but of its distortion: "Resistance against monopolization and domineering market tyranny cannot be simply equaled with the struggle 'against' the market, because such social resistance itself includes the efforts striving for fair competition in the market and for economic democracy."[114] Recall Habermas's notion of distorted

113   Wang Hui, *China's Twentieth Century: Revolution, Retreat and the Road to Equality* (London: Verso Books, 2016).

114   Wang Hui, "Debating for Our Future: Intellectual Politics in Contemporary China" (manuscript obtained from the author).

communication (distorted because of extra-linguistic power relations of oppression and domination). Wang seems to imply the notion of distorted market competition and exchange—distorted due to the external pressures of political, cultural, and social conditions:

> The movement of economy is always embedded in politics, culture, and other social conditions, so to strive for the conditions of fair market competition does not equal getting rid of [the] state political system, social customs, and any regulating mechanism. On the contrary, the perfection of market conditions aims to reform, limit, and expand these systems in order to create social conditions for fair interaction. In this sense, the struggle for social justice and fair market competition cannot be equaled with the opposition to state intervention. It rather requires Socialist Democracy, namely, to prevent the state from becoming the protector of domestic monopoly and multinational monopoly through the society's democratic control of the state.[115]

Here, one should remain a shamelessly orthodox Marxist. Wang underestimates the immanent logic of market

115   Wang Hui, op.cit.

relations, which subverts its own "fairness" and tends toward exploitation and destabilizing excesses. Wang thus seems to be fighting a straw man: *Who* is seriously claiming that the movement of economy is *not* embedded in politics, culture, etc.? Even Margaret Thatcher, the founding figure of "neoliberalism," was fully aware of this when she insisted that the economic measures imposed by her were just the first step in changing the entire sociopolitical question, up to our perception of human nature: "Economic problems never start with economics. They have deeper roots—in human nature and in politics. They don't finish at economics either."[116] This is why Thatcher explicitly grounded her politics in philosophy: "The philosophical reason for which we are against nationalization and for private enterprise is because we believe that economic progress comes from the inventiveness, ability, determination, and the pioneering spirit of extraordinary men and women."[117]

Consequently, Thatcher praised small and mid-level companies against big corporate monopolies. She also

116 Margaret Thatcher, "Speech to Conservative Party Conference," Margaret Thatcher Foundation, October 10, 1975, https://www.margaretthatcher.org/document/102777.

117 Mark J. Perry, "Tribute to Margaret Thatcher," AEI, May 4, 2020, https://www.aei.org/carpe-diem/tribute-to-margaret-thatcher/.

believed her responsibility was to "prevent the state from becoming the protector of domestic monopoly and multinational monopoly." And even Jinping would have agreed with this: His new round of reforms is not anti–Deng Xiaoping; his target is the new big corporate monopolies. However, when Wang claims that we should "prevent the state from becoming the protector of domestic monopoly and multinational monopoly *through the society's democratic control of the state*,"[118] we should add that if this is Socialist Democracy, then it never really existed. Can we seriously claim that in today's China society has democratic control of the state? We can, but on one condition: that we assume that there is equality between society and the (Communist) Party. In this sense, we can say that the Party controls the state on behalf of the people, but what we for certain do not have in today's China is society's democratic control of the Party. This isn't necessarily a negative feature: There are good arguments for the claim that China avoided the chaotic disintegration of the USSR in the early 1990s because Xiaoping's economic liberalization did not succumb to the temptation to abandon the Communist Party and pass power over to a

118   Wang Hui, op.cit.

Western-style multiparty democracy. Wang advocated for social democracy with the caveat that it should be grounded in the Asian civilizational traditions and function as a social order with strong participation of the people. Along these lines, Wang rejected the claim that Mao and Deng pursued opposed political options, and that Jinping simply stands for a (limited) return to the Maoist hardline. Instead, he argues that they are all part of a continuous emancipatory process that began with Sun Yat-sen and led up to the Chinese intervention in the Korean war, and more recently, Chinese attempts to unite with Taiwan. The narrow Western view misses this key point, seeing only a struggle between "Western liberal democracy" and Communist "totalitarianism" in this process.

Wang perceives Europe as a collection of nation-states (even the EU tends to become a big nation-state), while he praises China as a unique multicultural civilization. But is not China's tendency toward a strong united nation-state with tight control of minorities (Uyghur, Tibetan) extolling patriotism as its supreme value? Is not today's EU much more multicultural, with growing regionalism and minorities demanding more autonomy (in Scotland, Wales, the Basque Country, Catalunya)? And with no tendency to impose a privileged language (with Brexit, even the English loses some of its hold)? Another Pan-Asian Leftist argument is that in Europe and the U.S., capital reigns directly, with the state apparatus mostly just serving it (even the support of Ukraine is done to support the military-industrial complex), while in China the movement of capital is subordinate to state control and regulation. But isn't Europe, in regard to socio-economic rights, still far more "objectively Social Democratic" than China, a state much more exposed to popular pressures?

One should also highlight the tension between an official ideology and its actual implications, well beyond the standard Marxist point that, in capitalism, liberal freedoms and rights justify exploitation and domination. In a recent debate, a Muslim friend of mine argued that Islam offers far better protection against corruption and financial profiteering than Western capitalism, grounded in the Protestant individualist ethics. The Quran prohibits interest rates and demands a portion of profits are given to the poor. It treats private wealth not simply as an individual's property, but as part of a social wealth that the individual must distribute for the common good. Sounds nice, but then why is corruption much more rampant in Muslim states than in the Protestant Scandinavian countries?

Wang and other Leftist Pan-Asians use the term People's War in reference to Asian emancipatory movements—military operations that go beyond the state army and involve a large strata of civil population, like farmers and workers. Examples include the Chinese Revolution, the Vietnam War, and the Korean War. However, doesn't the term fit perfectly with what goes on in Ukraine after Russian aggression? The Ukrainian Army's activities are combined with local initiatives, self-organization, and forms of improvisation, like small personal drones used for reconnaissance and bombings. Russian forces are clearly not waging a people's war— hundreds of thousands fled the country to avoid being mobilized, and Russia had to resort to mercenaries and prisoners. When China sent "volunteers" to help North Korea (after the U.S. Army intervened on behalf of the UN to enable the South to survive), these volunteers were simply regular army units. It's the same with North Korea offering Russia 800,000 volunteers to help it fight against Ukraine.

We should thus qualify our earlier statement: China and Russia are also hypocritical in their own ways. Their proclaimed respect for national differences is a fake, they clearly prefer particular sociopolitical options around the world (mostly authoritarian ones). When

Putin claims that Islamic states and the monarchies of the Persian Gulf have the right to choose their way of life, he ignores the inner antagonisms, tensions, and struggles in these countries (like everywhere else). As the protests in Iran demonstrated, these inner antagonisms open up space for another universalism that is opposed to imperialist universalism: the universalism of the struggle for emancipation, of the global solidarity of all those oppressed.

Slavoj Žižek is one of the most prolific and well-known philosophers and cultural theorists in the world today. His inventive, provocative body of work mixes Hegelian metaphysics, Lacanian psychoanalysis, and Marxist dialectic in order to challenge conventional wisdom and accepted verities on both the Left and the Right.